CONDITIONS OF FREEDOM

CONDITIONS OF FREEDOM

Being the Second Lectures of the Chancellor Dunning Trust, delivered at Queen's University Kingston, Ontario, 1949

★

JOHN MACMURRAY

Professor of Moral Philosophy,
The University of Edinburgh

FABER AND FABER LTD
24 Russell Square
London

First published in mcml
by Faber and Faber Limited
24 Russell Square, London W.C.1
Printed in Great Britain by
Latimer Trend & Co Ltd Plymouth

FOREWORD

*

The Trustees of Queen's University invited Professor John Macmurray to deliver the second series of Chancellor Dunning Trust Lectures. The theme of the freedom and responsibility of the individual in our modern society is so important that it can only be adequately treated if approached from more than one point of view. Professor Macmurray's treatment of the subject is challenging and arresting, for it makes a demand on us with all the validity of the Christian imperative.

These lectures made a deep impression on the audiences. They are now available, in this printed form, to be studied by a still wider audience.

R. C. WALLACE

Principal's Office,
Queen's University.

PREFACE

The three lectures here published were delivered under the auspices of the Chancellor Dunning Trust at Queen's University, Kingston, Ontario, in January 1949. The first two lectures stand as they were delivered. The third has been considerably enlarged. This lecture was originally condensed to a point which made it somewhat difficult to follow; and in preparing it for a wider public it seemed advisable to remove, so far as the subject would allow, the danger of misunderstanding. In expanding it for publication, I have added nothing to its substance, and have changed the form of the argument hardly at all.

It is the duty of the Chancellor Dunning Trust lecturer to promote understanding and appreciation of the supreme importance of the dignity, freedom and responsibility of the individual person in human society. There can surely be no more urgent task in our time, nor one, I venture to think, more difficult of adequate performance. Men whose minds are dazzled by the splendours of a scientific technology and whose pulses echo the rhythm of the machines are unapt to understand or to appreciate the things that belong to our peace. Dignity, freedom and responsibility are inseparably bound together. Without freedom we have no dig-

9

PREFACE

*

The three lectures here published were delivered under the auspices of the Chancellor Dunning Trust at Queen's University, Kingston, Ontario, in January 1949. The first two lectures stand as they were delivered. The third has been considerably enlarged. This lecture was originally condensed to a point which made it somewhat difficult to follow; and in preparing it for a wider public it seemed advisable to remove, so far as the subject would allow, the danger of misunderstanding. In expanding it for publication, I have added nothing to its substance, and have changed the form of the argument hardly at all.

It is the duty of the Chancellor Dunning Trust lecturer 'to promote understanding and appreciation of the supreme importance of the dignity, freedom and responsibility of the individual person in human society'. There can surely be no more urgent task in our time; nor one, I venture to think, more difficult of adequate performance. Men whose minds are dazzled by the splendours of a scientific technology and whose pulses echo the rhythm of the machines are unapt to understand or to appreciate the things that belong to our peace. Dignity, freedom and responsibility are inseparably bound together. Without freedom we have no dignity. Without responsibility we have no freedom. The threat to our freedom comes not from without but from within; from a lowering of our sense of human dignity and from a growing effort to escape responsibility. It comes even more, perhaps, from an intoxication with power, and an unmeasured faith in organization. These have their place, and can yield us much that is desirable. Yet they are hard to reconcile with freedom; and they easily rob us of our responsibility and our dignity. The world of the spirit has its own laws of causality, which cannot be broken with impunity. To learn these laws and to obey them is our business. If we neglect it, we shall certainly lose both dignity and freedom, and we shall have no just cause of complaint.

I have sought, therefore, to discharge my trust, and to honour the memory of a distinguished Chancellor, by discussing, to the best of my ability, the fundamental conditions of human freedom. To do justice to such a theme is too hard a task. I can only hope that I may have fulfilled the function of a good sign-post by pointing in the right direction.

I wish to thank the trustees of the Chancellor Dunning Trust for the honour of the invitation to deliver these lectures; and all those who made my visit to Queen's an inspiration and a delight. To the staff and to the students of the University I owe a debt. In the fellowship they offered I received more than I could give. Where all were generous and kind it would be invidious to name any; but I cannot refrain from expressing a special gratitude to the Vice-Chancellor and Principal, Dr. R. C. Wallace. It was a privilege to be associ-

PREFACE

ated, however slightly, with his unstinted and self-effacing service to his own University, and to the wider community of Canada which his University adorns.

JOHN MACMURRAY

Edinburgh,
12th July 1949.

CONTENTS

CONTENTS

*

13

I

THE RELATIVITY OF FREEDOM

*

There can surely be no necessity, in any country of the British Commonwealth, to prove the importance of freedom, or to persuade men to a belief in freedom. At most we require, at times when we are distracted by special difficulties or when things are going too easily for our good, to be reminded of the price that our fathers had to pay for the freedom that we enjoy, and of the duty we owe to our children for its preservation and its increase. In a very special sense freedom has been the primary objective of our Western civilization from the days of the Renaissance. Little by little, and often desperately, freedom has been won and extended; built into habits of common life and buttressed by institutions. In the crowded history of our modern achievement there is a wealth of good things that we have made our own and made available to mankind for ever. Yet all of them have their roots in that freedom which is our most precious achievement; and if that soil loses its sweetness and its health, they too will wither and die. It is not our power—whether of knowledge or of technique or of machinery—which matters, either as the glory of our past or as the guarantee of our future, which now has become the future of mankind. It is our faith in freedom. If that faith is lost then all is lost; and our power will turn to our destruction, and but for the grace of God, to the destruction of the whole world.

It seemed right that I should begin by reminding you of this before I discuss the relativity of freedom; lest it might seem that I were engaged in an effort to limit and to qualify what should remain for us and for all men an absolute and unconditional obligation. This is not my intention. Freedom is, I am assured, the pearl of great price for which, if we are wise, we shall be prepared to sell all our possessions, to buy it. The ancient and wide-spread belief that the supreme good of human life is happiness, for all its persuasiveness, is false. Freedom has a higher value than happiness; and this is what we recognize when we honour those who have been ready to sacrifice happiness, and even life itself, for freedom's sake.

There is a sense in which freedom is absolute. It is the sense in which freedom is the defining character of Man; the property which sets us apart from the rest of creation and fixes a gulf between us and the highest of the animals. This absolute freedom is simply our capacity to act—not to behave or to react, but to form an intention and seek to realize it. To act is to be free. As agents we are concerned not with the past or the present but with the future: not with what exists, then, but with what does not yet exist; not with matter of fact but with matter of intention. In action we stand between the past and the future, between what has been done and what is still to do. The present is merely the point of action.

When we turn back from action—when we reflect—we see what has been done; and this is the world that exists, the world of fact. So we find this world of existence completely determined. We have no power anywhere to alter it. It is what it is, because it is as it has been determined. This utter determinateness of all that we find in existence excludes freedom, we know. But this is no more than the knowledge that time is irreversible, and that we cannot alter what has already been determined. When we return to action we turn to the future, away from what exists, from what is determined, from what is unalterable. The future is the field of freedom, and when we act, we determine the future. For to act is to determine, and the agent is the determiner. To assert determination and deny freedom is to assert that we never act; that no man ever, in very truth, *does* anything; and the assertion that our actions are determined is itself an exercise of freedom which denies itself.

Such an argument, however, while it demonstrates the absoluteness of freedom, is far too abstract to satisfy even those whom it convinces. So soon as we move towards a more concrete statement, the relativity of freedom appears, and with it the paradox of freedom, from which all fruitful thinking must take its beginning. 'Man is born free, yet everywhere he is in chains,' said Jean-Jacques Rousseau. That is a famous historic formulation of the paradox. It is expressed in religion in the story of the Fall of Man, and by theology in a doctrine of Original Sin. It is experienced by all of us in the conflict between conscience and impulse. Perhaps the simplest expression of the paradox lies in the difficulty we find in being ourselves. All other creatures are what they are, always and inevitably. This is their determinateness; so that they can be known through and through by observation and inference. But our human nature eludes us. There is a gap between the reality of our being and its empirical expression, which teases us perpetually; and those who know themselves best are most conscious of the difference; so that, as St. Paul has put it, 'it doth not yet appear what we shall be'. We are and yet we are not ourselves: and in this is our freedom. Our own human nature lies always beyond us as a goal to be aimed at, an objective to be fought for and, perhaps, taken by storm. So freedom is at once absolute and relative: absolute, because if we were not free we should not be human at all; relative, because this freedom lies always beyond our present achievement as the goal of our existence. It is at once the Alpha and the Omega of our humanity.

But I have expressed this truth all too optimistically, following a tradition that has been hard hit by the disasters of our recent history. I have conjured up a picture of Man eager in the pursuit of freedom, seeking to be himself through the difficulties of circumstance and the obstacles of material conditions, free always in spirit, but thwarted by the necessities of a natural world to which freedom is alien, and which recks nothing of spiritual values. We would be free; we strive for freedom; but there is that in the nature of the world which thwarts our effort and brings our struggle to failure. This is an ancient doctrine, of which Plato is, for us, the fountain-head. Yet I am bold enough to think that it is

false, or at best a dangerous half-truth. We flatter ourselves too much when we imagine that we love freedom
and strive wholeheartedly towards freedom. On the con-
trary; there are few things that we fear so much. No
doubt we find the *idea* of freedom most attractive; but
the reality is another matter. For to act freely is to take
a decision and accept the consequences. The free man
is the man who takes responsibility for his own life before God and his fellows. Is it any wonder that when we
are faced with the challenge of freedom, our fear is
usually more than a match for its attractiveness; and
that we seek, for the most part, to escape the demand
that it makes upon us? This, at least, is my experience;
and that our capacity to deceive ourselves in this matter
is of extreme subtlety. I see history, in its concrete reality,
not as Man's struggle to win his freedom in a world that
frustrates his efforts; but as a record of the twists and
evasions by which men seek to escape from freedom in a
world which thrusts it remorselessly upon them. The
determination which oppresses us is not the opposite of
freedom; for what is determined is that Man shall be
free.

Here then is the paradox of freedom. We are free to
choose between freedom and security. This choice is not
voluntary nor is it once for all. It is compulsory, and it
is perpetually recurrent. It is a real choice: for we can
make either freedom or security our goal. Yet there is an
element of illusion about it, too. For the demand for
security is the reflection of our fear; while freedom is the
expression of our own reality. If we use our freedom to
escape from freedom we frustrate ourselves: if we persist

in this choice we destroy ourselves. If we aim at security we aim at the impossible, and succeed only in multiplying the occasions of fear, and magnifying our need for security. There is no security for us except in choosing freedom. For our insecurity *is* our fear, and to choose freedom is to triumph over fear.

So, in the concrete experience of human life and in the complex processes of human history freedom is not absolute, but relative. It is not something that we possess, but something we may choose; not something we inherit but something we may strive towards if we have the courage. It has to be earned and paid for, and often the price is high. We can have more or less of it; yet it is never a secure possession; it is easily lost; and if we think to rest in the freedom we have achieved, then it begins to diminish, for it is an expendible asset. Only in the struggle to increase it can we hope to maintain the freedom we have already achieved.

In its immediate simplicity freedom is the ability to carry out our chosen purposes; to do what we please. So the problem of freedom is contained in the question, 'Why can we not do as we please?' To this question the moralists have given us various answers—because God forbids it; because it would not be good for us; because it would not be right. Yet all these answers assume that it is natural that we should not be free; and how can that be true if freedom is the essence of our nature? If we cannot do as we please—and undoubtedly we cannot—then something is wrong somewhere. If our freedom is only relative, then there are obstacles in the way; and the struggle for freedom is the effort to remove the obstacles. If we cannot do as we please—and we know that this is constantly our situation—should we not ask what prevents us from being free, and how we can remove, or at least lessen, the hindrance to our freedom. The increase of freedom is an enlargement of the field in which we can do as we please.

When we approach our question in this attitude, we notice that the relativity of our freedom depends, clearly, upon our power to do what we desire to do, so that an increase in our power will mean an increase in our freedom. But our freedom also depends upon *what we want to do*. For it is no limitation upon a man's freedom that he has not the power to do something that he has no desire to do. We can increase our freedom, therefore, by limiting our desires, without any change in the means of action at our disposal. The free man is the man whose means are adequate to his ends. We can gain freedom by increasing our power while our ends remain constant, or by limiting our ends to the means at our disposal. Let us call these two limitations of freedom the technological and the moral relativities respectively.

It is characteristic of our Western civilization in the modern period that it has sought the increase of freedom chiefly and increasingly along the technological road, through the increase of power. I need not enlarge upon this nor upon the astounding success which has crowned the effort. But there is much to be said about the other means to freedom, which concerns itself with the modification of our desires; with operations upon ourselves and not upon the world. In the first place, let me remind you that this way of seeking freedom has gone out of fashion. It used to be the main road along which men sought their freedom—through religion and the moralization of human nature; through the release of the soul from the tyranny of vain desires; through self-examination and the cultivation of contentment. We have forgotten these things. We have come to think them unnecessary, or at best the business of a peculiar minority, who feel themselves called to be saints. The other means to freedom, the increase of power—for what is power but the means of doing things?—has been so successful, the increase in our power so spectacular, that we have come to think that of itself it could provide us with all the freedom we could use; that in the long run there are no limits to our power to do what we desire.

This concentration on one of the variables is as disastrous as, for us, it is natural. The increase of power is an increase of freedom only if our demands remain relatively stable. But this is what they never will do if left to themselves. Plato saw this more than two millenniums ago. In the *Republic* he pointed to the fact that though animal desires can be easily satisfied, desire in man is insatiable. For when the natural needs of men are supplied, new desires appear for more elegant and more complicated satisfactions, until the resources available are too few for the demands upon them: and in this he found the origin of war. The very spectacle of increased resources breeds a corresponding proliferation of desires; and if this process is uncontrolled, desires always grow faster than the power to satisfy them; for their increase is rooted in the creativeness of the imagination. If, then, we double our resources while we treble our demands upon them we do not increase our freedom. We diminish it. There is no need for astonishment that the vast increase of our resources in the last generation has gone hand in hand with a loss of human freedom. The two variables—the moral and the technological—must both be considered. Self-control is as imperative as the control of nature if freedom is to be increased or even maintained.

There is a widespread tendency to believe that our desires, along with the whole emotional side of our nature, is so much natural fact; irrational, and so incapable of modification. We can suppress our desires, we think; we can refuse them the satisfactions which they demand. But they change, if they do change, of themselves, obeying some natural law, but not the dictates of any rational decision. This is not so. There is an essential relation between our desires and our knowledge, and I would draw your attention to an aspect of it which is closely bound up with the relativity of freedom. We cannot desire what we know to be impossible of attainment. We can wish, no doubt, that what is impossible were within our reach, but we cannot make it the object of desire and the objective of action. We do constantly aim at the impossible, and so frustrate our freedom; but not if we know that it is impossible. We can even deceive ourselves into thinking possible what we really know—or could know if we would let ourselves —is not. But we cannot effectively desire what we clearly know to lie beyond the limits of possible achievement. For this reason it is one of the conditions of freedom that we should seek a clear conception of the limits of human power. It is a hard lesson for us to learn, for the increase of our technical resources has made us arrogant. Great as it is, that increase is only relative: it has to be measured against the vastness of the field in which we have no power at all. Until we recover our sense of proportion, until we recognize our creatureliness and our dependence, we shall continue to frustrate our freedom by desiring what we cannot attain, and by using our resources for our own destruction. Humility is the handmaid of freedom. It is the meek who inherit the earth.

Our discussion of freedom is still, however, too abstract and ideal. The most important aspect of its relativity has still to be noticed. Human freedom can be realized only as the freedom of individuals in relation; and the freedom of each of us is relative to that of the others. Man is dependent upon the world, of which he is a part; but every man is even more intimately dependent upon his fellows in the interrelation of men which constitutes human society.

It is a commonplace that human life is social. But like many commonplaces it is imperfectly understood, and often ignored in practice. The fact that men live normally in groups, like many of the higher animals, is of relatively little importance here. It does not touch the essence of the matter. It is not the fact that men live together that counts, but the knowledge of this fact, and the intentions to which this knowledge gives rise. What constitutes the humanity of the human group is the consciousness of each member that he belongs to it; and the intention, which pervades all his activities, to realize his membership, even if it must be, at times, in anger and revolt. It is the life of the *individual* which is a common life; and we can only be human in community. Even our secret thoughts are elements in a life that we share with our fellows; for their truth lies in their reference to a common world; and if they lose this reference they become the fancies of insanity.

I hope to take up this central theme in my final chapter. For the moment it is enough to remind ourselves that our freedom, as individuals, depends upon the co-operation of others. We are fed and clothed by our fellows. The whole apparatus of our life is provided by others. That the system of co-operation is impersonal and indirect makes it no whit less real. Nor is it merely the material resources which we use at every moment that are the gift of others. The language we speak, the thoughts we think, the ideals we cherish and pursue are only partially our own. We have them from those who went before us; and the forms they take in our private minds and mouths bear witness that they are symbols of a life that is shared.

I shall not labour what is so obvious whenever we attend to it. But it has two corollaries to which I shall direct your attention. In the first place, it is the fact that we are dependent on others for our freedom which both explains and justifies our habit of contrasting freedom with slavery. Where there is no freedom, we turn instinctively to seek the tyrant who is its suppressor. The freeman, we think, is he 'who serveth not another's will'. Now, as I have tried to show, there are other conditions of freedom than the interference of those who are more powerful than we. Nature herself imposes her bondage upon us; and even more important—we fall victims to our own fearfulness. Yet both these threats to our freedom are mediated through our dependence upon other people. The tyranny of natural necessity appears as the pressure of the economic system on our social relations; and the fears that constrain us are fears of what others will think or say or do. Even the fear of death, which seems so individual, and which is the symbol of all human fear, is the psychological equivalent of the terror of isolation, of being cut off irretrievably from the community to which we belong.

I have suggested that we cannot desire what we know to be impossible. If we stood alone against the forces of Nature, the limits of our power would be easily learned, and our desire would shrink within the compass of the attainable. So we should be free. But because we are social beings, dependent upon the co-operation of our fellows, possibility has a double meaning for us. A great deal that is possible in the nature of things is made impossible if the others will not co-operate with us in its achievement. More than this—if the others are determined that we shall not have what we desire, they can always refuse it to us, however simple a thing it may be, however easily attainable with their goodwill. It is this situation which sets the problem of human freedom. For it defines a wide field of possibility which is conditional upon the extent and the quality of social co-operation. Within this field we can aim at possibilities which are open to us if others will share them; and we can lose our freedom when they will not. So the essential conditions of freedom are social; and the simplest answer to the question, 'Why can I not do as I please?' is, 'because other people won't let me'.

There is a second corollary of our interdependence which is less widely recognized, and which seems to me the most important of all. No man can compass his own freedom for himself. He must accept it as a free gift from others; and if they will not give it to him he cannot have it. This is a law of freedom. Against it our fear and our pride beat themselves in vain rebellion. If we struggle to achieve our own private freedom we merely frustrate ourselves and destroy its possibility; for we cannot free ourselves from our dependence upon our fellows. That this is not so is one of the great illusions of a sophisticated society. When we profess our faith in freedom we often mean only that we want to be free. What value, what honour is there in such a miserable faith? Which of us would not like to do as he pleases—if only he could escape from his fear of the consequences? To believe in freedom, in any sense worthy of consideration, is to believe in setting other people free. This is to some extent within our power, and it is the greatest service we can render; even if it must be, at times, by the sacrifice of our own. In giving freedom to others, we have a right to hope that they in turn will have the grace and the gratitude to give us ours. But of this we can have no guarantee.

In the nexus of personal relationship which is our common life, the enemy of liberty, the great inhibitor of free action, is fear. I do not mean the direct fears that have an immediate danger before them; for these are natural and call only for a natural courage. But there are deep and pervasive fears in us which have primitive roots and which are projected upon the future by our imagination. If they gain control, they turn us upon the defensive, so that we see danger everywhere and spend our energies in the attempt to secure ourselves against the future. We feel relatively safe only within the circle of familiar habit, where action is automatic. Before the unusual, the foreign, the unknown, we feel the need of protection and defence; and because of our intimate dependence upon our fellows, we fear one another most of all.

The mechanisms of self-defence which we develop to serve our fear of other people are of two types, one negative and one positive. The negative is a mechanism of withdrawal, through which we provide ourselves with the illusion of independence. We make our relations with others as indirect and as automatic as possible, so that they can be stereotyped in a technique which prevents too close or intimate a contact. Since this subjects our co-operation with others to a rule, we lose our freedom of action. But we can compensate for this, in idea, by achieving a freedom of the mind, a spontaneity of the imagination. In this way we produce in ourselves a feeling that we are independent, that we are free from the others. For we meet them only impersonally, and their demands upon us appear only as the pressure of a mechanism of institutions, which we call Society and which fades insensibly into the order of Nature, governed and guaranteed by eternal laws which we cannot change.

Our other type of defence is the struggle for power.

We meet our fear of others by an attempt to make ourselves stronger than they, so that we can compel their co-operation in our purposes. We seek some position of privilege, some superiority over our fellows that can force their service. We set up if we can, between us and our fellows, instead of the relation of fellowship, the relation of master and servant. This is the origin of all tyranny, from the petty tyrannies of family and workshop to the major but often more tolerable tyrannies of the dictators and conquerors. This defence also is illusory and self-defeating. For it springs from fear, and depends for its success upon the inculcation of fear. The master is dependent upon his slaves and helpless without their service; if they lose their fear of him he loses his hold upon them. The more they fear him, the more he must fear them, for he has wronged them and they are justified in rebellion. So the fear he inspires increases his insecurity and his need of power for his defence, in a vicious circle that can end only with his own destruction. He spreads fear like an infection through the circle of his relationships, and poisons the springs of freedom both for himself and for his victims. Though he may indulge in a frenzy of grandiose activity, his ends are negative and destructive. Nothing creative can be accomplished through fear; and no power, however impressive in its extent, can avail us against the inevitable. For the saints and for the philosophers this is an ancient lesson. Yet we have had to hear it told again in our time as the story of Hitler's Germany.

These then, so far as I can discern them, are the general principles which govern the achievement and the increase of human freedom at all times and in all circumstances. Beyond these, however, our freedom is relative to the conditions in which we live and to the particular problems of human relationship which they set for us. In the history of social development circumstances change and the problems which they set change with them. Any substantial alteration in the social conditions of human life resets the problem of freedom and demands a new effort and a new solution. So it comes about that often men seek to escape from solving the problem of freedom which is their own by spending their efforts in the defence of the freedom they have as a gift from past generations. There is great danger of this for us. The freedom of to-day must be fought for and won in the conflicts of the present; and if we fail in this we shall lose, and we shall deserve to lose, the freedom of yesterday. But this is a new theme which needs a new start. I shall make it the subject of my second chapter.

CONTEMPORARY CONFLICTS

The primary condition of freedom, to which all other conditions are related, lies in the character and the quality of human relations. This was the effective conclusion which we reached in considering the relativity of freedom. We have to start from the fact of our interdependence. We need one another, and none of us is sufficient unto himself. The extent to which we achieve freedom in this common life depends upon the extent to which the constraint of fear has been removed from it; the extent to which the co-operation it demands is positively or negatively motived.

When we look back upon the history of social development, we see that there are two ways in which freedom has been achieved and extended. These two ways are the social correlates, so to speak, of the two variables we noticed in the relativity of freedom—the moralization of desire which controls the ends of action, and the control of the means of action through the increase of power. Considered in relation to society these appear as the socialization of ends and the socialization of means respectively. The first defines the field of religion; the second the field of politics, using both these terms in the widest possible sense. The religious effort seeks to eliminate fear by deepening and extending the sense of brotherhood, fellowship and communion among the members of an interdependent group. This is the inner or spiritual way of achieving unity and so fulfilling the condition of freedom. So far as it succeeds it binds us together in sharing a common life so that we belong together, and find ourselves with common values, common objectives and a common way of life. The religious conquest of fear seeks freedom through friendship.

The political way, on the other hand, aims at freedom through justice. The type of unity it seeks is external. It accepts men as they are, with their fears and their self-centredness, and concerns itself with guaranteeing a system of co-operation for common ends which will be fair to all, and which will prevent at least the grosser tyrannies to which the use of power so easily gives rise. It is this political road to freedom with which we shall concern ourselves in this chapter; and, in particular, with the direction it must take in the conflicts of our own time. But before we turn to the problem as it faces us to-day, there are two general remarks which I should like to make. The first is this. These two ways of securing freedom are not alternatives, either of which can reach its goal by its own success. They have a relative independence; but each needs the other. Of the two the religious effort is the more fundamental, because it seeks to deal directly with the desires and motives which govern the relationships of men. Politics, on the other hand, must deal with actual situations, and maintain a working co-operation whatever the motives of the co-operating members may be. This is a more negative task. It aims at mitigating the effects of fear rather than at its elimination. Clearly the task of politics becomes easier and its success becomes fuller in proportion to the inner unity of the society for which it prescribes. The degree to which the members of a society are conscious of their fellowship decides the shape of the task which is set for politics. If fear and enmity are rife, the justice which can be secured will be difficult to attain and meagre in its quality. If they increase beyond a certain point justice and even co-operation may become impossible.

The second remark concerns the relation of politics to power. We are apt to think that politics is the exercise of power, and that the State works through compulsion and constraint. The fact which gives colour to this opinion is that alone among institutions the State has the right to use force to secure obedience to its commands. This fact, however, is easily misunderstood. The purpose of the State is the elimination of the use of force in human intercourse. We arrange, therefore, that if force *must* be used, it shall be used *only* by the State. Nor do we stop there. We go on to secure that it shall be difficult for the State to use force; that it shall be used, even by the State, only after due process of law, and only as a last resort when all else fails. The intention of politics is not the use of force, but the elimination of force and the achievement of freedom through justice.

But this must be qualified by recognition of the difficulty of the task. The interdependence of men in society is a fact, and the system of co-operation which it entails is necessary. So the first task set for any government is

33

to maintain effectively the system of co-operation. The penalty for failure is universal distress and social collapse. If co-operation can only be secured by compulsion, then compulsion must be used. We must co-operate, and if we will not freely, then under constraint. Abuses of power by governments are always possible, and have to be guarded against; but we are apt to blame the individuals who perpetrate them far beyond what is reasonable. The true sources of such misuse are always to be found in the social conditions, in the character of the social co-operation, which make the large-scale use of the power of government essential. Dictatorship is always undesirable, it is always a confession of failure and a threat to freedom. But history shows us that men can make it inevitable; and that sometimes it has been beneficial, and has been exercised in the service of justice and of freedom. When we consider the threat to freedom in our own time, the widespread attack upon democracy, and the rise of dictatorships, let us remember this. Democracy as we know it is not, of itself, a guarantee of freedom; far less is it to be identified with freedom. Freedom has other and profounder roots. The English people prided themselves upon their freedom long before democracy, as we know it, had been thought of. In the conditions of our time, and, I believe, for as far ahead as we can see, democratic institutions are an essential condition of political freedom. But they are not the whole story.

Let me state at once the general thesis which I wish to develop, so that you may know in advance where I am leading you. The conflicts of the contemporary world are the symptoms of a change in the form of human society. We are living through the first world revolution. Probably we are yet in its early stages, and its completion may lie a long way ahead. What we have long called 'the modern world' is coming to an end, and we are beginning a new chapter in the history of human development. The change is of such an extent that every country is involved in it. It is so profound that there is no level of human experience which is untouched by it. If we seek its causes too locally or too superficially we shall fail to understand it, and our efforts to cope with it will be unsuccessful, leaving us with a sense of helplessness and despair. But if we grasp our situation in its entirety and have a courage that can match it, we shall realize that it is full of hope and opportunity, and that it moves towards a great emancipation. For its goal is the unification of the world in a common life.

To explain this fully would be much too large a task. It would take us back to the origins of Western civilization at least. I should try to show how the driving force behind the process of our history is the impact of Christianity upon Europe, and the slow penetration of the Christian spirit through its habits of life and thought. For in spite of temporary appearances, I am convinced that the influence of Christianity, properly understood, was never more widespread nor more effective than it is to-day. But we must limit our range at least to that phase of its development which began in the changes which dissolved the culture and the economy of the Middle Ages, and ushered in the modern world.

The core of that great change lay in a transformation

of moral attitude. In the Middle Ages, as in all customary societies, the idea of rightness was associated with
the past and so with the authority which acted as the
guardian of tradition. The right way to do anything was
to do it as it had always been done. The wise men of old
had discovered, or had had revealed to them, what was
right to do and to believe. The Church was the custo-
dian and interpreter of tradition. Men defied the tradition, of course, but they knew that they were doing
wrong. In the Renaissance, however, and increasingly
thereafter, we find men associating the idea of rightness
with the future, and believing that the right way to do
things is to do them better than they have been done
before. From this new moral outlook spring the distinguishing characteristics of the modern period—the
special preoccupation with freedom as the right of the
individual to live his own life in his own way. For this
means freedom of individual thought and individual
conscience, freedom to experiment, to try out new ways,
to doubt and criticize tradition. In such an attitude
there is imbedded the idea of a better way of life and a
better form of society, to be sought for and established.
Progress, as a conscious ideal, had begun.

The effort to live by such a faith, however, soon revealed the poverty of our resources. Society was shackled
to customary routine by the necessities of life. When all
must labour from dawn till dusk to provide the bare
means of existence, only a privileged few can strike out
new ways for themselves; and they only at the expense
of the multitude of their fellows. The vision of social
freedom had to remain a vision. The resources for its

realization must first be accumulated and the realization itself postponed. The modern world has cherished the idea of freedom as its goal; while in practice it concentrated its efforts upon the increase of power. So the modern period of our civilization became the age of accumulation; and its governing principle is the law of accumulation, that what is gained shall be used to gain more of the same. In the economic field this has made it the era of capitalism, when wealth is invested and not expended; used to gain more wealth. In the political field it has been the period of the increase of political power as a matter of public policy, so that power achieved is utilized for a further expansion of power. In the field of reflection it has been the era of the creation of science; of that type of knowledge upon which the techniques of power and control can be established: and here again the principle holds, that knowledge shall be pursued for its own sake, and used for its own increase.

In the accumulation of power there are two phases. The first is simple accumulation, a mathematical process of adding more and more. But this by itself has limits; for mere increase in weight either of numbers or of bulk soon becomes unwieldy and hinders rather than helps. The second phase is the increase of power by organization, so that the increasing mass of resources can be utilized. The two periods of our modern history follow this pattern. The dividing line between them is, in the economic field, the transition from merchant capitalism to industrial capitalism; in politics the democratic revolutions; in science, the creation of the sciences of the organic, after the mathematical sciences had been set on secure foundations. The great change is even more revealing in the field of culture. In art and literature, the classical tradition yields to the romantic movement, with its concentration upon Life and Nature, and in philosophy the mathematical conceptions of the Cartesians are challenged by the new philosophies of the organic.

In the period of history which lies immediately behind us, the struggle for freedom has been directed to the organization of the institutions of political democracy. This has had the effect, natural but dangerous, of identifying freedom in society with the existence of representative legislation based on popular suffrage. I should be the last to deny the importance of the institutions of democracy as instruments of freedom. But I am concerned to insist that they do not of themselves confer freedom upon those who live under them. The constitution of Russia, and its political organization, are admirably democratic in form, but the substance of freedom, so far as I can see, is still to seek. And not a little of the danger to democracy in our time comes from the disappointment of large numbers of people who expected more from the extension of the franchise than it could possibly give. The nineteenth century was not the heyday of democracy, but of its preparation. It was the period in which, step by step, the political machinery of democracy was constructed, and this constructional task was completed, in Britain, only in the twenties of this century, with the grant of universal adult suffrage, after the first world war. The democratic period lies ahead of us, in the use that we make of the free institutions which have so recently been completed. In a word, it is not the institutions of democracy which confer freedom upon men but the essential justice which can, if we will, be secured by their means. What made them essentials was the great loss of freedom which accompanied the industrial revolution. For industrialism produces swift and continuous change in the social system of human co-operation, and continuous shifts in the balance of power within it. If justice is to be maintained, this involves continuous adjustments in the law. The effect which universal suffrage secures, if it is rightly used, is not that the opinions of all shall count—never in my life have I had the good fortune to cast my vote for a candidate who was elected—but rather that the needs and difficulties of all classes shall be considered in the process of seeking justice through the modification of the law.

While at home the fight for freedom was building the institutions of democracy, two other movements were setting the problem of freedom which we have to solve to-day. Together they began, in different ways, to forge links between the peoples of the world. The first was the expansion of overseas and international trade, and the movements of colonization which went with it. The second was the missionary enterprise of the Christian churches. Of these two, the religious expansion is the slower and the less spectacular, but I have little doubt that future historians will reckon it the more significant of the two. But it is the economic expansion with which we are concerned at the moment. The effect of it was to extend the co-operative interdependence of men in society until it included the whole world. The power and wealth of the advanced nations increased rapidly, but at the expense of a rapidly increasing dependence, for food and raw materials, upon peoples beyond their borders. At the outbreak of war in 1914, mankind had already become one society of interdependent, co-operating individuals. War was the result of this; in a real sense the inevitable result. But because we were unaware or only vaguely aware of what was happening, war between civilized countries seemed incredible, and its outbreak was a profound shock, from which we have not yet recovered. The first world war proved the *de facto* unity of mankind as a single co-operative group; and it drove this interdependence into the consciousness of every person in the world who had acquired the habit of reading a newspaper. It is only if we start from this achieved economic unity of the world that the history of our own time can be understood, and that our contemporary conflicts can reveal themselves as a new chapter, and a potentially glorious chapter, in the long struggle for human freedom.

This universal society, however, was, and still is, inherently unjust. This was nobody's fault, or at least it is undesirable to ask whose fault it was. To seek a scapegoat is only a way of seeking to dodge one's own responsibility to put things right. What we need, in the present plight of our civilization, is to understand one another, and the maxim on which all human understanding rests is, 'Judge not, that ye be not judged'. The rule which I try myself to follow, and which I commend to you, is a simple one. When things go wrong blame nobody, not even yourself; but if you must blame some-body, blame yourself. For you are always partly to blame, however little, and your part in the blame is the part that you are responsible for putting right. The world society of which we are all now interdependent members is unjust. The process of industrialization has now done for the undeveloped peoples of the world what it did for the independent craftsmen and crofters of Britain in its early days. Its impact has destroyed the ancient institutions of their primitive custom; under-mined the social sanctions of their morality and their religion; and forced them, too often, to hew wood and draw water for alien masters. Yet their old customary ways were the instruments of their primitive freedom. We have destroyed it, in fact though not by intention, and created a world proletariat. In using the mastery that our power has given us to make them serve our needs we have become dependent upon them, and our dependence makes us afraid. If they hate us, if they be-gin to use our dependence upon them against us, and to refuse us the service we have need of, we have no reason for surprise and no just ground for anger. It would be an almost incredible generosity if they did otherwise. And yet, the incredible generosity of common men and women everywhere has sometimes brought tears to my eyes, and revived my hopes and with them my trust in common humanity, which is the working centre of any democratic faith.

I am not blind to the efforts after justice in inter-national relations which we have made: and I am not seeking to blame even ourselves. What is to the point is the fact that our interdependent world has no effective *instrument* of justice. Except in the direct relationships of life, there can be no justice without a law that can compel obedience if obedience is refused. When I buy a shirt I take the quality I desire at the cheapest price I can find. What else am I to do? Yet when I think of the numbers of my fellows who co-operated to produce it, how can I be sure that the saving of my money (which means the increase of my freedom) is not the effect of the exploitation and oppression of the Egyptian fellaheen who grew the cotton? Innocently I am involved in injustice to my fellows. If my relations with others are to be just, beyond the narrow circle of direct acquaintance, I must depend on a system of law which automatically adjusts the effects of my activities so that no injustice arises anywhere. Yet the one economic society of to-day is politically many, and there is no system of effective law which can secure justice for all its members in their dependence upon one another. It consists of a series of independent States, each with its own system of law to provide some sort of justice within its own borders. A system of independent sovereign States in a world which is economically one society *cannot* achieve justice and must destroy freedom. For it is a system in which each government must attempt to control the economy of the whole world in the interest of its own citizens. So each industrial State tends to take on the character of a gigantic business combine in economic competition with all its rivals; and there is no common authority to hold the ring, and to formulate the rules of what is fair and what is foul play. Is it any wonder that such a situation leads to world wars, or that when they come there are no inhumanities to which the struggling adversaries will not stoop?

It is often said that war settles nothing. This is a mistake. What seems to be true is that war under modern conditions never achieves the intentions of those who resort to it. It is the unexpected and unintended consequences of war which are important, and they settle a great deal. The victors of the first world war fought to defend freedom. In Britain we called it 'a war to end war' and 'to make the world safe for democracy'. In the distress and disillusionment which followed, we felt that it had been fought in vain; that democracy was less secure than it had been; that freedom was diminished and not increased. This was the case only in relation to the narrow range of our immediate hopes and purposes. That war, for the Western democracies, was an experience of disillusionment. But to be rid of illusions, if it does not break our courage, is a liberating experience; for it is a revelation of the truth. In a few years it transformed the consciousness of a great part of mankind by making us aware of our interdependence. The founding of the League of Nations was a momentous event in the history of freedom. It showed that men had discovered the true situation, and seen the conditions of freedom in our time—that liberty could only be defended by making it world-wide. It was the first attempt in history to create an instrument of justice for mankind as one society. That it failed was of less account. The new phase in the struggle for freedom through justice had begun; and it continues.

But this was not the only liberating effect of the first world war. It created the new Russia and the new China. The Russian revolution, long overdue, was the climax of centuries of fruitless struggle by the Russian peasantry against an oppressive, antiquated and inefficient despotism. If we are shocked at some of the immediate repercussions upon our own part of the world, and by the crudity and explosiveness of some of its manifestations, if it complicates our problems and threatens our security, we should not let our fears blind us to the major fact, that the Russian revolution has meant a great victory in the struggle for freedom to the peoples of one-sixth of the earth. Even more significant, in the long event, was the Chinese revolution, which gave China the testament of Sun-Yat-Sen, and the first sketch of a democratic polity. These two revolutions between them freed six hundred millions of the world's people from the yoke of an ancient bondage and set their feet upon the devious and dangerous road of progress. The first world war settled a great deal. From that time the security of our own freedom has been bound up with the increase of theirs. In the confusion and uncertainty which must accompany any sudden enlargement of horizons we have to defend the freedom that we have ourselves achieved. It is a trust we owe to the society of the future. We may not yield it to any threat of violence or seek to buy an ambiguous peace at its expense. But in our resolve to defend our freedom we have to see to it that it is not our power, our mastery, our privilege that we are defending, but in very truth our liberty. We have to remember the lesson of our own devious and doubtful past, that the struggle for political freedom is a struggle against privilege and domination. In the contemporary conditions, in the new struggle of an interdependent world for a universal freedom, we are the privileged nations, and the domination that must be yielded is our own.

In the uneasy interim between the two world wars, and in the second war itself, the problem of freedom was clarified and brought to a point. In the first place, the revolutionary character of the situation was exhibited. The Russian revolution was an ambiguous event. In one sense it was a belated national revolution for the overthrow of feudalism, to be classed with the French revolution in the West. But with the triumph of the Communist party it gained a new and international significance. For communism is a Western, not a Russian product; and it is international in its outlook and its objectives. Its triumph in Russia was widely felt to be a threat to the economic and the political structure of the Western democracies. As a national revolution it met and defeated, within its own borders, the counter-revolution of the adherents of the old regime. But this was followed by a new type of counter-revolution, in the Fascist movements. With the advent of Hitler to power in Germany there was created and organized, outside Russia, an anti-communist movement of great power; and the lines of conflict in the world revolution were consciously drawn.

A revolutionary situation is one in which a change in the form of society has become necessary. The existing institutions and habits of a society are incapable of solving the problems of the common life, and in consequence government loses control of the situation. History sets for such a society a problem of freedom which cannot be solved in terms of the existing forms of social organization, and which *must* be solved. The free choice between freedom and security is forced upon the interdependent group by the breakdown of the system of co-operation. The revolution may be achieved without bloodshed; but the fear and distress, the opportunities for injustice which such a situation must produce, make it likely that it will involve a civil war. The society divides and each side struggles for the mastery; and to the victor falls the task of constructing the new form of society which can solve the problem that has been set. If it fails, the revolutionary situation must continue, the struggle must be resumed; the problem will be reset for a new effort to its solution.

In the world revolution of our time there is one major divergence from the pattern. There is no effective world government against which rebellion can be directed. But that is incidental. The main lines of the pattern are the same. We have a world society of interdependent individuals, and what institutions it has to achieve justice are quite inadequate to its problems. So history has become catastrophic. The efforts we make to control the situation through modes of thought and action with which we are familiar make the situation worse rather than better. Think of the long series of international conferences in the 1920's on disarmament, upon economic and other world problems. Never in history was so much thought and care and goodwill mobilized behind human effort. Yet the failure of each in succession only

46

brought an increasing sense of futility and despair. At last Germany decided to give up trying, left the League of Nations, and set to work to solve her own problem by her own power. But the world was one society. It was a collapse in Wall Street that put Hitler in power; and each step in his career of private German nationalism brought the division of the world into two camps more close. In the war he initiated the logic of events showed clearly the unity of the world society; for it became evident that if he were to solve the problem of his own country by force of arms he could not stop short of the conquest of the world. These modern conflicts are civil wars in a world which is already one society, and in which the prize of victory is the task of creating, for the first time, the institutions of a political unity for the world, of building the instruments of world-justice. If we fail in this, the revolutionary situation continues, the unsolved problem is reset, and until the solution is achieved the conflict remains.

The second of the world wars is still too close to be seen in perspective. It has defeated an attempt to solve the situation by an appeal to force and conquest. It has kept open the road to a free and peaceful solution. It has brought a democratic liberty to the last great centre of human population in India after a long period of alien rule. One other of its effects is already plain. It has opened a new era in the struggle for freedom. From the time of the Roman Empire the story of human advance was the story of West European civilization. Until yesterday the tension that kept it in movement lay within Europe, as a tension between France and Germany.

To-day, western Europe is only one factor in a wider process. The initiative has passed beyond Europe. The East has claimed successfully its right to give as well as to take. The tension which governs the advance lies now between the United States of America and the Union of Soviet Socialist Republics. The field of its operation is the whole world. So, patently, the struggle for freedom has ceased to be the fight for the freedom of the individual in a local and separate national group and has become a fight for the freedom of the individual human being in the society of mankind.

These, it seems to me, are the conditions to which freedom is relative in our time. It may be that we of the West, who have advanced so far and grown so powerful, often at the expense of the rest of mankind, have now to learn that freedom is not our private possession, and to mark time while the others catch up with us. One thing we need, which is very difficult to achieve—the ability to see ourselves as only a part of a society which is universal; and, in our freedom, as the trustees of a possession which belongs of right to all men. We can preserve our freedom now only by sharing it. When we achieve this large perspective we can see that the increase in human freedom in the last generation has been enormous, both in its extent and in its speed; and that the difficulties that face us and which at times seem ready to overwhelm us, are in fact the consequence of this. It is the speed of the advance that alarms us. The whole world is on the march, terrible as an army with banners, and the goal is freedom. The future is big with promise; there is no reason for fainting or for despondency.

has ceased to be the fight for the freedom of the individual in a local and separate national group and has

3

FREEDOM IN FELLOWSHIP

★

1. Co-operation and Community

We have distinguished two main sets of conditions to which human freedom is relative.
The first touches the *means* of action. We must
have powers adequate to our intentions. The second concerns the *ends* of action. The intentions which we seek to
realize must themselves be possible. Underlying both is
the primary condition to which all freedom is relative—
the inherent sociality of human life. The power by which
we achieve our ends is a function of social interdependence, and its increase towards adequacy depends upon
the efficiency of the system of organized co-operation.
Equally, however, the possibility of the ends which we
seek is socially determined. For what one of us intends
may be incompatible with the purposes of others. The
demands made upon the available resources may be in
conflict, so that if one is achieved the other cannot be.
Sometimes, no doubt, this may mean only that the available means, though adequate for either, are too small
for both; and in such cases an increase in resources will
remove the incompatibility. But this is not by any means

D   49

always the case. The ends themselves may be in conflict. They may be *inherently* incompatible. In such cases freedom is lost. Even in the extreme case, where one party gives up his purpose without a struggle, he yields his freedom. But this is unusual, since it can only happen in the simplest cases where each party is directly and clearly conscious of the intention of the other. For the most part these conflicts of ends are mediated through the system of interdependence in which we live. They appear to us as impersonal obstacles which frustrate our efforts and whose origins we cannot trace. The conflict of ends gives rise to a struggle for power, and in this struggle the intentions of each party are perverted to securing victory over the other; and the resources available are used, and possibly used up, merely to reach a point at which the real intentions may be at length pursued. So freedom is destroyed. For while the conflict continues the adversaries must lay aside the hope of achieving their real intentions. Each must act for ends dictated by the other's opposition; and the victor, if there be a victor, regains his freedom of action with his resources impaired, and often reduced to a point at which they are inadequate to his original purposes. If, then, there is to be freedom in society, it is not enough that our resources should be adequate to our intentions. There must be a compatibility of ends. Our intentions must not merely be possible. They must be compossible with those of all the others. It is this demand for a compossibility of intentions which sets the problem of freedom in fellowship.

Of these two major conditions of social freedom, the

compossibility of intentions is the more fundamental. The economic system of co-operation for the production and increase of our resources has in itself no reference to freedom or to justice. Its regulative principle is simple efficiency; the best system is the one which produces the greatest quantity with the least expenditure of effort and resources. The unity it requires is not of persons, but of functions. The demand for justice in this co-operation, which is the proper aim of politics, is imposed upon it to safeguard the personal rights of all participants, and to prevent the sacrifice of freedom to mere efficiency. Justice, indeed, is a negative and external principle. It is negative, because its purpose is to set limits to the use of power. It is external, because it works through the subjection of everyone to rules. Yet it is a *moral* principle and rests upon an inner intention to secure that my own freedom shall not infringe the like freedom of other persons. It contains, therefore, a negative reference to the compossibility of intentions. Where intentions are not compossible, they shall be limited, by compulsion if necessary. The search for freedom through justice is itself a negative aspect of the effort to achieve a compossibility of intentions.

The achievement of justice in co-operation is relatively, but not absolutely, independent of the compossibility of intentions. In principle, whatever determines the ends of action must ultimately determine the means to these ends. The relative independence arises from the fact that the same means can be used to achieve diverse ends. It is possible, therefore, to amass resources without determining, in detail, the ends which they are to serve.

But there are limits to this independence. The efficiency of organized co-operation depends upon an orderly subordination of functions, and this must concentrate power in the hands of those persons or groups who exercise superior functions. If there is an incompatibility of intentions, those with superior power will achieve freedom at the expense of their functional inferiors. Justice, as the natural end of political organization, seeks to neutralize this effect, and to secure a fair distribution of freedom. It does this by means of a conception of *right*, which sets limits to the use of power, and to the inequality of its distribution. The exercise of freedom is the use of power to realize an intention. To limit the use of power is therefore to limit freedom. The principle of *right*, therefore, only arises where intentions are incompatible. It is pointless to limit the freedom of one person unless it is incompatible with the freedom of another; for where all are able to realize their purposes, however diverse these may be, everyone is equally free. Thus justice, originating in the necessity to regulate a *de facto* incompatibility of intentions, is itself concerned to secure a compossibility of intentions: but it does this negatively and externally, by determining, according to a rule, which intentions shall become effective in action.

Justice can be secured only through a system of institutions designed for the purpose of securing freedom. Yet these institutions, however perfectly designed, do not of themselves suffice to secure it. The effectiveness of democratic institutions depends upon how they are used. It is widely recognized that some peoples are more apt in their use than others. The British peoples have made excellent use of them. So have the Scandinavians. In Italy and in Germany democracy has had less successful results. In the South American Republics and in the Republic of China, the existence of democratic institutions has been even less successful in securing its avowed aim. These variations in effectiveness have generally been accounted for by reference to differences in national character. Though this is a vague and metaphorical notion, it has at least the merit of recognizing that the securing of political freedom depends on another factor besides democratic institutions and that this other factor is an inner and spiritual one.

The instruments of democratic freedom, then, can be used, more or less successfully, to secure their purpose. But they can also be used to defeat their purpose. In our own time we have witnessed, in Germany and elsewhere, the successful use of democratic institutions to overthrow freedom. We have seen the instruments of justice employed to establish tyranny and to maintain it. In face of this experience, though we may still insist that democratic organization is a necessary condition of freedom, at least in an industrialized society, we are debarred from counting it a sufficient condition. We are driven to inquire what this other factor may be which determines whether the instruments of freedom shall be used, and successfully used, for the purpose to which they were designed.

One difficulty which meets us when we seek to answer this question is the indefiniteness and ambiguity of the language at our disposal. Human nature, we have said, is inherently social. But the term 'society' is itself ambiguous. It covers any form of human association which is more or less permanent. Associations of human beings are of various types, however, and rest upon different principles of unity. Of these principles two are so radically distinct in type that their confusion has dangerous consequences, not in theory merely but also in practice. There is a type of association which is constituted by a common purpose. There is another which consists in the sharing of a common life. It is essential to our purpose to distinguish these by using different terms to refer to them; and I propose to use the terms 'society' and 'community' for this purpose. An association is, then, a 'society' when its members are united in the service of a common purpose; it is a 'community' when they are united in sharing a common life. The two principles of unity, clearly, do not exclude one another. A society may also be a community. But this is not necessarily so; and even where both principles are effective in the same group, they may be effective in very different degrees. But the principles themselves are radically distinct.

A society, in this sense, is a group of persons co-operating in the pursuit of a common purpose. The common purpose creates the association; for if the purpose should disappear, the society will go into dissolution. It also dictates the form of association; since the members must co-operate in the way which will secure the common end; and the ideal form for such an association is the form which realizes the common purpose most efficiently. Each member has his place in the group by reason of what he contributes, in co-operation, to the pursuit of the common end. He is a member in virtue of the function he performs in the group; and the association itself is an organization of functions. Thus, though the members are persons, and the group is an association of persons, the members are not associated *as persons*, but only in virtue of the specific functions they perform in relation to the purpose which constitutes the group; and the society is an organic unity, not a personal one. This organic, functional, impersonal character remains even where the common purpose is necessary and permanent. The co-operative association to provide the necessaries of life rests upon a common purpose which is not fortuitous, but universal and compulsory in human experience. The human societies which are constituted by such persistent and necessary purposes are still merely organic; they are functional and not personal associations. Their persistence and development, together with their compulsory character, give rise to the State, as a central organ for the co-ordination and regulation of the co-operative life of an interdependent group. The State is, thus, the central institution of society; that is to say, of the functional association of a human group. It is organic; not personal.

A community, on the other hand, rests upon a different principle of unity. It is not constituted by a common purpose. No doubt its members will share common purposes and co-operate for their realization. But these common purposes merely *express*, they do not *constitute* the unity of the association; for they can be changed freely without any effect upon the unity of the group. Indeed it is characteristic of communities that they create common purposes for the sake of co-operation instead of creating co-operation for the sake of common purposes. It follows from this that a community cannot be brought into existence by organization. It is not functional. It is not organic. Its principle of unity is personal. It is constituted by the sharing of a common life.

It might be objected that this in itself constitutes a common purpose to which community is relative. This is a common error in contemporary civilization, and it underlies the tendency to an apotheosis of the State. It is, indeed, the erroneous postulate of any thoroughgoing individualism. It assumes that the human individual is an independent, self-contained entity with a personal life of his own which he may or may not purpose to share with others. In fact, it is the sharing of a common life which constitutes individual personality. We become persons in community, in virtue of our relations to others. Human life is *inherently* a common life. Our ability to form individual purposes is itself a function of this common life. We do indeed enter into specific relations with our fellows in virtue of specific purposes of our own; and we must do so in order to realize, in concrete experience, the *common* humanity which makes us persons. But the sharing of a common life, in general, cannot itself be a purpose. It is our nature; and in sharing a common life we are simply being ourselves by realizing our nature. Community is prior to society.

We shall return to this essential issue later. For the moment we shall consider the practical effects of confusing the two types of human unity, as they have revealed themselves in contemporary history. For it was by his use of this confusion that Hitler was able to bedevil world politics for a decade. Not that he invented the confusion. He found it ready-made to his hand in the modern conception of nationalism. But the situation of the German people enabled him to use it with effect; and, I imagine, consciously.

Nationalism is a conception which identifies the idea of the State with the idea of nationality. The State is essentially territorial. It is a legal entity in the sense that the boundaries of its territory are the limits of its legal authority. It is a material entity—a piece of the land surface of the earth within which a single system of law is authoritative. Nationality, on the other hand, has no inherent reference to territory. Originally it is based upon natural kinship, and the idea of kinship clings to it even when the biological basis is no longer a matter of literal fact. A nation is a group of human beings who are bound together by a sense of kinship. The bond is a spiritual bond. The mere fact of kinship is not enough. If men are ignorant that they are racially kin, the mere fact will not bind them together. The belief that they are kin, even if it is scientifically without basis, will do so. Nationality, therefore, as a unifying force in human association, is a psychological, not a geographical, fact. The 'kinship' which constitutes it is symbolic, even when it has a real biological basis. Essentially it is constituted by the consciousness, in its members, that they share a common life, a common experience, a common tradition. Among the many factors which may combine to produce such a 'national consciousness', one of the most effective is the sharing of a common language. A common religion would seem to be more powerful still;

in the case of the Jews, for example, it has been able to preserve the sense of kinship for centuries in the absence of almost all other factors.

To be effective, nationalism requires the coincidence of these two factors—the territorial and the psychological. Where all those who are united by a sense of common nationality happen also to reside within the boundaries of the same State, the task of government is, of course, much easier. But there is no logical relation between the two principles of unity, and their coincidence in fact is fortuitous, depending upon the accidents of history. With the development of world transport, and the increase of migration, it becomes less and less likely that the coincidence required by nationalism will in fact be found. The attempts to produce it artificially by a compulsory exchange of populations, which we have witnessed after both world wars, are barbarous and unnatural. Nationalism, with its dogma of the so-called right of national self-determination, rests already and will rest increasingly, if it persists, upon an unconscious atavism in the human mind. So long as it persists, it is a menace to the peace of the world. It can be dissolved only by dissociating its two components—the idea of citizenship, depending upon territorial residence, and the idea of nationality.

In Germany the coincidence of the two components of nationalism was only approximate, and the element of national consciousness was the stronger of the two. There has always been a primitive and sentimental mysticism clinging to the German idea of 'das Volk'—the people; a sort of legendary tribalism which found symbolic expression in the idea of 'blood and soil'. The political unification of Germany, on the other hand, came only very late; imposed forcibly by the military power of Prussia, and necessitated by industrialization. The German State had to be constructed out of a loose confederation of principalities. The basis for this construction was the sentiment of an organic, an almost biological unity of the German Folk. The task was to find a legal and therefore a territorial organization which would embody and express this sentiment of unity. But in the case of Germany, the attempt to combine the two components of Nationalism—territory and national sentiment—sets an insoluble problem. It is not possible to draw a line on the map which will enclose all the people who are bound together by the sentiment of German nationality. In other parts of western Europe— in France, in Italy, in Spain, in Britain, for example— there are natural boundaries, or where the boundaries are artificial, they have been so long defined that there has been time for the sentiment of nationality to grow up within them. With Germany this is not so. Even her western boundary, for a Germany seeking to construct a national State, is ambiguous. It has been defined for her, by other nations, without too much regard to national sentiment. Alsace-Lorraine, in particular, is problematic, and also of great industrial importance. But the eastern boundary has always been fluid, and along it the intermixture of peoples makes any determination artificial. It is complicated, too, by religious distinctions. Protestant Germans are mixed with Orthodox Slavs, Roman Catholic Germans with Roman

Catholic Slavs in Poland, Catholic Germans with Protestant Slavs in Bohemia, where the natural territorial
boundary of the mountains fails conspicuously to coincide with the limits of German sentiment. Austria herself is indubitably German, but until 1918 was bound
up in the Austro-Hungarian Empire with a heterogene-
ous mixture of peoples, with outlying German settle-
ments in Transylvania and the Trentino. On the south
again there are the Germans of Switzerland. Thus any
attempt on the part of Germany to construct her political and territorial unity on the principle of national
self-determination could only lead, as it did, to confusion, catastrophe and war.

It was this situation which Hitler exploited so skil-
fully. Internally he completed the process of unifying
Germany proper as a single, organic political unity,
which had begun in earnest after the Napoleonic wars.
Then, taking his stand upon the principle of nationality,
as the leader of the German 'Volk' he claimed the allegiance of all Germans everywhere to himself, for the
task of creating the single, all-inclusive German *State*.
This is the meaning of the Nazi slogan, *Ein Führer, ein
Volk, ein Reich*—one leader, one people, one kingdom. It
is important to realize that in taking this line, Hitler
was only pushing the dogma of the right of national
self-determination to its logical conclusion, and in the
process revealing the inherent irrationality of nationalism. The attempt to realize the German ideal involved,
of necessity, a threat both to the unity of sentiment and
to the territorial integrity of other States. Germans outside the borders of Germany could not give loyal allegi-

ance both to the German Reich and to the countries of their residence; nor could they be included within extended German frontiers without including at the same time large numbers of non-Germans. Any possible solution, short of abandoning the attempt, could only be imposed by force. But the day is long past when localized territorial adjustment can be achieved by an appeal to arms. Industrialism has linked the peoples of Europe and of the world in a network of interdependence; and political organization is ineffective when it is not integrated with its economic basis. In fact, under modern conditions, the German appeal to war to achieve the demands of nationalism could only be successful if Germany could unify Europe, and ultimately the world, under her own suzerainty, by military conquest.

Under Hitler's leadership, Germany carried nationalism, with its principle of self-determination, to its logical conclusion. By doing so, Germany has proved the bankruptcy of nationalism as a principle of political organization, and has set us the task of overcoming and transcending it. From now onwards nationalism and freedom are incompatible. Their association since the French Revolution, with one another and with the idea of progress, is accidental. In principle, modern nationalism is atavistic; it is a relapse into primitive tribalism; an attempt to reinstate the original organic unity of primitive society as an ideal for civilization. In rejecting nationalism, we are rejecting that worship of the primitive, that glorification of 'nature', with which the Romantics, from Rousseau onwards, infected modern European culture. We are refusing to be misled, by biological analogies, into substituting an 'organic' society for a human community: and in doing so we are returning to the straight path of civilized development.

It is characteristic of primitive society that the two principles of unity, fellowship and co-operation, define the same group of people. The original kinship-group, from which all subsequent forms of human association are derived, is based upon blood-relationship, upon descent from a common ancestor. Kinship is the basis both of co-operation in work and of fellowship in community. This primitive group is the truly 'organic' society. It is as close to the animal world as human life can come. The artificial element of rational construction is present only in embryo. There is a common life in which all the kin have their part; and reflection is limited to the consciousness of the common life and the expression of this consciousness in the rituals of primitive religion.

The development of the primitive group towards civilization inevitably dissociates the two bases of unity, so that they no longer define the same group. For this effect, the institution of slavery is decisive. In any slave-owning society the spiritual unity of fellowship is limited to a part of the co-operating group. The slaves are included in the society as co-operating members; they are excluded from the community of fellowship. From this point onwards it is rare to find a society in which both principles of unity define the same group of persons. The institution of an agricultural economy, and the settled life that goes with it, introduces territorial boundaries,

and gives an impetus to the growth of property, and
particularly of property in land. In consequence, residence within the territory of the group appears as a
qualification for membership, and ownership of land
within its boundaries is a qualification for *full* membership of the community. The development of trade between independent territorial groups complicates and
diversifies both types of unity. Co-operation passes beyond the limits of territorial and so of legal control; and
some members of the group are linked in friendship with
strangers. This process is well exemplified in the history
of ancient Greece, and it produced the situation which
created the imperialism first of Macedon and then of
Rome: and in the city states of Greece, as in Hitler's
Germany, it gave rise to the reactionary ideal of 'self-
sufficiency'—the vain effort to re-establish the primitive
coincidence of co-operation and fellowship within the
territorial limits of political independence.

In the Roman Empire the attempt to combine the
two principles of unity has been given up. Its unity is a
unity of organized co-operation within which religious
and cultural toleration allows older unities of fellowship
to maintain themselves and new forms of fellowship to
develop autonomously. The Romans created in this way
the modern idea of the State, as a unity of society based
wholly upon law and administration, and so providing
a framework within which co-operation can be organized and developed. The State, so conceived and constructed, has a pragmatic justification only. It is not
concerned with culture, with unities of fellowship, except in so far as they threaten to disrupt the system of

co-operation which it maintains. Its business in this field is the negative one of 'keeping the peace'.

Within such a system of administration, provided it is efficient, there tends to grow up a sentiment of loyalty to the institutions it maintains, and a sense of unity with all one's fellow-citizens. This inner shadow of the external system of co-operation is real enough, and can under suitable circumstances and by suitable methods provide a strong motive for common action. But since it is impersonal in its nature, and dependent upon self-interest in the efficiency of the system of government, it has not the binding force of a sense of fellowship which is direct and personal. In the history of the Roman Empire, therefore, we find attempts to strengthen its inner unity by appeals to religion; first, in the deification of Rome, and of the Emperor as the personal symbol of Rome; and finally by the adoption of Christianity as the official religion of Rome. So there was created, in the society of the Roman Empire, what has remained the ideal pattern of social unity for West European civilization. The two principles of human unity are recognized as functionally separate. Church and State are charged with the care of the inner and the outer unity of society respectively.

In this final phase of the history of the Roman Empire the external, territorial, legal unity is already realized. The task of the Church is, as it were, to transform the unity of co-operation into a unity of fellowship. After the collapse of the Roman Empire the situation was reversed. The Church survived the State, and it fell to the Church to create the unity of Western civilization anew, with the ideal inherited from the Roman Empire as its guiding principle. In this case it was the spiritual unification of western Europe which came first. What was created was Christendom—an inner unity of fellowship through a common religion. The task which remained was to create a corresponding political and administrative framework for Christendom so that it might be also an effective co-operative unity. This political unification of Europe was never effectively realized. The Holy Roman Empire remained a form and a hope which failed to achieve substance. When the medieval world gave way to the modern, the new, protestant forms of religion shrank within the framework of the new independent states and modern nationalism was born.

When, therefore, we turn to the problem of our own day, which is, as we have seen, the achievement of an effective world unity, we should bear in mind both principles of human unification. We should remember the relative dissociation of fellowship and co-operation in the process of social development, and the variety of possibilities which their interrelation affords. In particular, we should recognize and oppose, in our own modes of thought and speech, the atavism which infects our modern tradition, and which has been so powerfully reinforced by the influence of biological and evolutionary metaphors. The organic society, with its fusion of co-operation and fellowship on a basis of blood-relationship, lies not at the end, but at the beginning of history. It is what we are moving away from. The patterns of unity in fellowship no longer coincide with or correspond to the political patterns of economic co-operation. Nor is it either possible or necessary that they should.

FREEDOM IN FELLOWSHIP

The facts of the contemporary situation are against nationalism. Great Britain is, and has long been, a political unity of different nations. The sentiment of national unity among its citizens attaches to Scotland or Ireland or Wales or England, in the first place; and this fact has proved not a source of weakness, but of strength. This British differentiation of the cultural from the political unity had its main source in the historical accident by which a Scottish king inherited the English throne. It was confirmed by the failure of the English attempt—totalitarian in conception—to force episcopacy upon Scotland. Scotland remained free in fellowship, with her own type of established religion and her own distinct type of law. The solid and characteristic British resistance to totalitarianism is closely related to this fact and to the historic experience which has flowed from it. An epidemic of militant nationalism would not consolidate, but disrupt the political unity of Great Britain. From this experience, too, flows the peculiar unity of the British Commonwealth of Nations. The bond of unity in the Commonwealth is purely spiritual. It is a unity of fellowship, unfettered by compulsory legal or economic bonds, which is yet extremely strong in spite, or should one not say, because of its freedom. The structure of this inner unity is extremely complex and fluid, as any unity of fellowship must be. It is composed of an interlacing network of particular and diversified loyalties and friendships. Its strength lies in this; and any attempt to impose a comprehensive legal and political unity upon it would destroy it.

When we look at the inner structure of the United

States of America, the same diversity appears, though on a different pattern. Here a single legal and political unity, federal in structure, encloses a great diversity of nationality, race and tradition. American nationality, like British nationality, is a formal and legal conception, which depends ultimately upon residence within the territory covered and defined by Federal law. The diversity of origin in the United States is so recent and so palpable that even a mythological sense of blood relationship is out of the question. Ties of nationality, tradition and culture link large sections of the American people to the various countries of Europe; and the unities of fellowship that have been developed between them in the new world link the nations of Europe in a new unity of European culture beyond their borders. The effectiveness of this inner and spiritual unity has been clearly demonstrated in our own lifetime. In two great wars it has triumphed over the economic self-interest of the United States, and brought its armies to Europe to save the threatened freedom of the European continent. Today it provides the mainspring of the generous and self-sacrificing aid which makes possible the reconstruction of European life, and tends powerfully in the direction of a political federation of European nationalities.

We recognize these facts when they are pointed out to us, though perhaps we do not apprehend their general significance. When we think about the future, and plan for our salvation, we tend to ignore them. When we refuse a world unity which would subordinate to one nation all the other peoples of the earth, we cannot but recognize that the diversity and intermingling of nation-

alities, races and cultures make any principle of nation
ality out of date as a basis for complete political freedom
It is rather an irrationality to be contended with; an
obstacle to be overcome. So we ignore it and all it im
plies and concentrate upon purely political and economic organization. We find ourselves, in consequence
contemplating a world state. My contention is not tha
such a structure is impossible or inconceivable, but simply that it could only be achieved, as things are, by the
sacrifice of freedom. A world state, in the present condition of world society, would necessarily be totalitarian. The strength of communism depends in great
part upon the fact that its conception of society has n
relation to the principle of nationality. It provides a
theoretical basis for an international, world-wide unity.
A communist unification of the world is therefore a real
possibility. A third world war, in my opinion, whatever
its outcome, would make it a certainty. But freedom
would disappear for a long time in this process, not because communism intends to destroy it, but because it
thinks and plans exclusively in terms of co-operative
unity, in economic and political terms, and ignores,
when it does not actively oppose, the human unities of
fellowship which alone, in the last analysis, make freedom possible. It seeks freedom through justice alone;
and subordinates the freedom of fellowship to the patterns and the exigencies of economic co-operation. It is
this that is expressed in its doctrine that culture is a
superstructure to an economic foundation. It is this that
is symbolized in its antagonism to religion.

2. *The Nature of Fellowship*

Up to this point we have been considering the distinction between co-operation and fellowship as types of human unity, and the tendency in history to their differentiation. We must now turn our attention to the nature and the significance of fellowship itself. Here lies the centre of the problem of freedom and the only hope of its resolution. This conclusion follows directly from our starting point. Freedom is the defining character of human existence. Our capacity for freedom makes us persons. But this capacity has to be realized in the empirical experience of living and in the actual conditions, which vary from generation to generation, in which our life is set. The core of the problem must lie, then, not in the more impersonal aspects of human relationship, but where they are most total and most personal. Political freedom is abstract and impersonal. It abides in the character of co-operative relationships, and these are compatible with personal indifference, and with motives of the most varied kinds. Enlightened self-interest will serve, at least within limits, to sustain the co-operative effort, especially if it is supported by a common enmity. But personal freedom is incompatible with such motives. It can be achieved only in fellowship. Indeed, the extent and the quality of such political freedom as we can achieve depends in the last resort upon the extent and the quality of the fellowship which is available to sustain it. Conversely, the unity of co-operation, which is the care of politics, has significance only through the human fellowship which it makes possible; and by this its validity and its success must be judged.

Any type of human unity must be realized under conditions; and in consequence it can be fully realized only where the conditions provide for its complete expression. The instances in which the structure of such a unity can best be seen, are those in which the conditions allow for its complete and at the same time its simplest realization. Now unities of co-operation and unities of fellowship differ markedly in this respect. The possibilities of organization, upon which the first type depends, require a considerable complexity and permanence to manifest their full nature. Other conditions being equal, indeed, the larger and more persistent the group, and the more fundamental the purpose which its association serves, the more scope there is for the structural characters which constitute its unity to reveal themselves clearly. The structure of an organized society is best realized where it secures an effective unity of co-operation in a complex differentiation of functions. There are, of course, manifold instances of co-operation between two people, and the bare bones of the structure of co-operative unity are present in them. But they are present only in germ, and not evidently. It requires a more developed form of association to display the mature structure of a society.

In the case of a unity of fellowship, however, the typical instances are precisely those in which only two persons are involved. The reason for this is plain. Any unity of fellowship is personal. It is a unity of persons *as persons*; and each member of a fellowship enters it with the whole of himself and not in respect of a particular interest which he happens to share with others. The conditions necessary to realize fully what is implicit in such personal relationships, and to express their meaning and character clearly, can hardly occur except between two persons. 'Two is company, three is none,' says the proverb. The presence of a third party limits at once the possibility of full intimacy and self-revelation. In a group the full realization of the potentiality of fellowship is limited, and the larger the group the severer must be the limitation. This does not mean that in the larger communities fellowship is less real, or that it differs in its essential character. In the larger fellowship the full intention remains latent and potential, as it were, and is fully expressed only in the direct relations of its members, each to each.

A passing stranger may stop to help me lift a load which is too heavy for me; and in so doing he creates a unity of co-operation between us which is as simple as it is evanescent. Yet this is rather an expression of fellowship, a gesture of friendship, than a co-operative unity; and it is very difficult to imagine a persistent co-operation of two persons for a common purpose which excluded friendship as its basis. A pure unity of co-operation, or an approximation to such a unity, can hardly exist unless the great majority of those involved are only in indirect and impersonal relation with one another. For it is, in essence, a merely functional relation. In a unity of fellowship, however, the reverse is the case. The more it involves organization, the less fully are the constitutive relationships expressed. In the activities of a great church, for example, the communion of its members can only be *symbolized* in its services and ritual. It can be *realized* only in the direct fellowship of the persons who constitute its membership. To understand the nature of fellowship, therefore, we must consider it first in its fullest manifestation, in the mature friendship of two human beings. Our central question is, then, 'What are the structural principles which constitute the unity of a friendship?'

We can begin to answer this question negatively, by contrasting the unity of friendship with any functional unity. In the first place, it is not constituted by a common purpose. It may arise, of course, in the beginning, out of such a purpose; and it will certainly involve common purposes and co-operation to achieve them. But it is not *constituted by them*. A relationship which is constituted by a common purpose is simply not a friendship. Friends are necessarily interested primarily in one another, not in what each can achieve through the assistance of the other. In the second place, and because of this, friendship cannot be *organized*. It is not based upon, nor does it express itself in a functional differentiation, a division of labour. Since friendship will certainly generate common purposes, it may give rise to organization, but this is not of its essence. In particular, friendship does not involve, as any co-operative unity does, the subordination of one person to another. This is clearly incompatible with the nature of the relationship.

These two major contrasts enable us to state in positive terms the two major constitutive principles of fellowship. The first is *equality*. Friendship is essentially a relation between equals. This does not mean that 'only equals can be friends'. To think this is to fall into the error of defining human existence in functional terms. To assert human equality is not to say that two or more people are equivalent for this purpose or for that, in one respect or in another. It is not to say that they are equally clever, or equally strong, or equally good. Personal equality does not ignore the natural differences between individuals, nor their functional differences of capacity. It overrides them. It means that any two human beings, whatever their individual differences, can recognize and treat one another as equal, and so be friends. The alternative is a relation between an inferior and a superior; and such a relation excludes friendship. It is a relation of master and servant.

The second constitutive principle of friendship is *freedom*. This means, in the first place, that the unity between two friends cannot be imposed. It can neither be established nor maintained by force. It is entirely, and throughout its whole duration, dependent upon the free activity of the persons concerned. It means, in the second place, that it provides for a complete self-expression and self-revelation which is mutual and unconstrained. As in the case of equality, it is here that we must look for the essential meaning of human freedom. In other aspects freedom is achieved only negatively, as an absence of constraints imposed from without. Friendship reveals the positive nature of freedom. It provides the only conditions which release the whole of the self into activity and so enable a man to be himself totally, without constraint. It is in this sense, in particular, that freedom is a constitutive principle of friendship. In its absence, any relation between persons must involve an inner constraint, and each must act a part and be other than his complete self.

Here again we meet, in its full concreteness, the paradox of human personality with which we began. Our reality as persons is always in us, and yet always beyond us. We are and are not ourselves. Any human fellowship is both matter of fact and matter of intention. Equality and freedom are *constitutive* principles of friendship, but they are also ideals to be achieved in friendship. It is the mutual intention to treat one another as equals and to be free in relationship that makes us friends; and the presence of the intention in the relationship means that it is already, to some extent, realized. Yet it is never completely realized, not merely because we fail to achieve it, but also because it 'grows by what it feeds on'. Each partial or temporary realization creates new possibilities of further and fuller realization.

We should note also that equality and freedom, as constitutive principles of fellowship, condition one another reciprocally. Equality is a condition of freedom in human relations. For if we do not treat one another as equals, we exclude freedom from the relationship. Freedom, too, conditions equality. For if there is constraint between us there is fear; and to counter the fear we must seek control over its object, and attempt to subordinate the other person to our own power. Any attempt to achieve freedom without equality, or to achieve equality without freedom, must, therefore, be self-defeating.

The democratic slogan—liberty, equality, fraternity —embodies correctly the principles of human fellowship. To achieve freedom and equality is to create friendship, to constitute community between men. Historically, however, it is infected with the error we have just considered. It was enunciated as a *political* objective, to be achieved by legal and administrative reform. In consequence, it involved the confusion of community with organized society, and implicitly set territorial limits to human fellowship. Conversely, it endowed the political state with moral and spiritual qualities which imply its absoluteness, and contain the seeds of totalitarianism. Certainly, the organized co-operation of human beings is for the sake of the fellowship of the common life, and in this sense the freedom and equality of brotherhood is the end to which the State is a means. But it is an indirect end. The State, as such, being a centre of organization within territorial limits, can only provide at best the material conditions in which fellowship can flourish and through which it can manifest itself.

These, then, are the structural principles of the type of human unity which we have called fellowship, and which constitute the persons whom they unite a community. It remains to discuss the ultimate ground of fellowship, and to show why, in the nature of things, fellowship takes precedence of co-operation. We live in a society of co-operation because we need the assistance of others in the pursuit of our human purposes. Why do we enter into fellowship with one another?

The answer to this question is that in no other way can we be ourselves. But this answer, simple and final though it is, is hardly self-explanatory. Yet if by 'explaining' it we mean getting behind it to something more ultimate, then it cannot be explained. It is like asking for an explanation of the fact that material bodies gravitate. We can only say that it is the nature of bodies to gravitate; that if they did not they would not be *bodies*; that if the material universe were not united by gravitation, there would be no material universe. So the forces that unite men in fellowship express the ultimate nature of humanity. We can say that we enter into fellowship because this is our nature; that if we did not we should not be human; that if mankind was not united in this way there would be no mankind. There is, however, a difference in the two cases. The nature of bodies is a matter of fact. They always and necessarily are themselves. But, as we have seen, human nature is not merely matter of fact. It is also matter of intention. What makes us human is the intention to realize our humanity. We may mark this difference by saying that human nature is self-transcending.

But if we cannot 'explain' this, we can exemplify it; and in doing so we may start from that aspect of it which is most familiar, because so much of the energy of philosophizing has concentrated upon it. I refer to the nature of knowledge. Thought is self-transcending, or to put it in a more familiar way, thought is *objective*. From a purely subjective, or psychological point of view, thinking is merely a process of ideas in our minds, a 'stream of consciousness'. But this misses the real point. It is of the essence of thought that it refers beyond itself to something other than itself. It is 'about' something. When we really think, we are seeking to realize the truth about an object. Because of this, philosophers have said that we are rational beings. This 'rationality' is our capacity to know the world 'outside us', and we do this by forming *true* ideas 'inside us'. So it is our nature, as thinking beings, to know what is other than ourselves. We know the world in which we live; but again we do not know it except in so far as we succeed in making our ideas about it true. This aspect of our human nature has to be realized intentionally, in a never-ending effort to conform our thoughts to the nature of the objects we think about. If we are to realize our rational nature in this way we must be interested in the object, and not in ourselves, and be concerned with its nature rather than our own. For if we are not interested in the object, we shall not make the effort to know it; while if it is our own thoughts in which we are interested, we shall shape them to our own liking and think 'as we please'.

One other aspect of this self-transcendence in knowledge is important for our purpose. It is the fact that if we are to think truly we have all to think the same thing. Knowledge is common. There is only one common world, and the truth about it is valid for all alike. Though each of us must think his own thoughts for himself, so far as we think truly we are bound in a community of knowledge, and there is one world for all of us. Thought realizes itself in the community of truth.

All this is commonly recognized. What is overlooked is that these characters of thought are not confined to the life of knowledge. They are partial and limited expressions of the self-transcendence which is the defining characteristic of human personality as a whole. Knowledge belongs to the reflective life of personality; and it is only one aspect of that. There is also an aesthetic reflection which is concerned with beauty, as knowledge is concerned with truth; and it too has its own peculiar objectivity and self-transcendence. But it is the life of action that is primary, and in an important sense it contains and completes the reflective activities. Consequently it is in action that the full nature of personality is revealed, and in particular in the springs of action, the dynamic motives, which determine and direct our conduct.

There are two and, I believe, only two fundamental motives which determine the dynamic structure of the personal, as distinct from the merely organic life. They are *love* and *fear*. The one is positive, the other negative. As personal motives they are general, pervasive and permanent, determining the dynamic pattern of character, in contrast to the organic impulses, which are intermittent and successive. These two ground-motives are differentiated by the organic impulses on the one hand and by the variety of their objects on the other; and in their own interplay, in which fear inhibits love, and so frustrates the positive activities which love intends. This interaction gives rise to a third motive which is general but derivative, namely, hatred.

We are faced here with a difficulty of language, particularly in regard to the meaning of the term 'love'. It is clearly the proper term to use, since it is the name we give to the motive which creates and sustains friendship, and all the forms of human fellowship. The variety of its applications is an advantage, rather than a difficulty, so long as these all remain personal. The ambiguity which has to be guarded against is the confusion of love with sexual impulse. The identification of love with sex, which is now so widespread, and which has received scientific sanctification in the psychology of the Freudian school, is merely an instance of the error which identifies the personal with the organic, and which we have had to expose again and again in other connections. But it is the most disastrous, because the most intimate and effective instance. It is not too much to say, perhaps, that unless this form of our most radical error is overcome, it must destroy our civilization. This is not the place to discuss this issue. We are concerned only to avoid ambiguity. It must suffice, therefore, to point out that, in principle, there is no essential relation between love and sexual attraction, even in cases where both are operative, and where the one is easily mistaken for the other. There can be love without sexual attraction; indeed this is normal in personal life. There can be sexual attraction without love, though this is an abnormality which is very common. Love is a personal motive; sex is an organic and functional impulse. When, therefore, we use the term 'love' to denote the positive motive which sustains every form of human fellowship, and which manifests itself most fully in the direct relationship of two persons, we must be clear that no reference to sex is implied.

The same ambiguity is present in the term 'fear'. The word is used indiscriminately for the organic impulse and the personal motive. Animal fear is a specific reaction to a particular danger which is directly sensed. Personal fear is the permanent and pervasive motive producing a defensive attitude and dictating a defensive policy. It inhibits the actions which would realize our positive intentions, and substitutes negative intentions, either of self-concealment or of aggressiveness. In its proper subordination to love it sustains the activities of reflection, and introduces the element of caution into our practical activities, preventing us from 'acting without thinking'. It is in this sense that fear is the negative ground-motive of personal activity.

Love, as the positive ground-motive of personal activity, can best be defined as the capacity for self-transcendence, or the capacity to care for the other. Love is *for the other*: fear is *for the self*. In actual experience, of course, both motives are operative together; and either may dominate the other. Where fear is dominant, the self becomes the centre of reference, and all commerce with the external world is for the sake of the self. Conversely, when love is dominant, the centre of reference lies outside the self, and the activities of the personal life are for the sake of the other. Now since fear is in its own nature inhibitory, its effect is to limit the spontaneity of the self and to curtail its freedom in action. The farther its dominion extends, the more the self is confined and limited in the expression of its nature. Indeed, beyond a certain point it must destroy the capacity for self-transcendence in the self and produce insanity. This is why the psychologist finds some form of fear, some phobia, at the root of all mental derangement. Clearly, therefore, our capacity to realize our nature and to be ourselves in full achievement depends upon the extent to which love is the dominant motive of our total activity.

FREEDOM IN FELLOWSHIP

It is one of the traditions of philosophy that the *differentia* of human nature is Reason. We have discovered now that it is Love, as the capacity for self-transcendence, which is the defining character of the personal. What, then, is the relation between the two? This is partly a question about language, and different people will decide it differently. We may take Reason as the proper name for whatever it is that distinguishes man from the animals, and then we shall have to identify Reason with Love. Or we may prefer to retain the common identification of Reason with the capacity for knowledge, in which case we must surrender the view that Reason is the *differentia* of human nature. But the essential point, which belongs to the substance of the issue, is to realize that our capacity for knowledge is a particular and limited expression of our capacity for self-transcendence. The rationality of thought is its objectivity, and the motive which sustains this objectivity in our thinking is our interest in the object for its own sake, which alone can shape our ideas to the nature of the object instead of to the nature of our own desires. To seek the truth is, in fact, to care for the nature of the object, within the limits of our intention to know it.

This, however, is merely reflective. When we act as persons, we act with knowledge, and so in terms of the nature of the object. Rational action has its own objectivity, even when we treat the world simply as material for our own satisfaction. The ultimate aim may be egocentric; yet our ability to compass it depends upon the truth of our knowledge of the objects we use, and upon our willingness to conform to the laws of *their* structure and behaviour. In such a case, however, our human capacity for self-transcendence is only partially and imperfectly expressed, and unless the object is itself personal this must be so. Only another person can elicit a total response in action, of such a kind that the self-transcendence of every aspect and element of our nature is expressed and fulfilled. This is the implicit intention of all fellowship—the complete realization of the self through a complete self-transcendence. If this intention could be realized in an actual instance, the self would 'care for' the other totally; in action and in both modes of reflection, intellectual and emotional. 'I' would think, feel and act *for* 'you', in terms of 'your' nature and being. In this way, and only in this way, could a personal being achieve and experience a complete objectivity, a complete rationality, a complete self-realization. The ground of friendship is, therefore, the inevitable need we have to be ourselves. It is our nature, as persons, to live *in the world* and not in ourselves; to have the centre of intention and realization outside ourselves, in that which is other than ourselves. The basic condition of this is that we should enter into fellowship, that we should love the other. So love may be defined as the complete affirmation of the other by the self: and since to be completely oneself is to be completely free, fellowship is the basic condition of freedom.

To complete this exposition of first principles we must add that the essential condition for *realizing* fellowship is a mutual reciprocity. The individual cannot achieve freedom in fellowship unless the other person does so too. I may love another person and find that my love is not returned. In such a case my love for the other remains only an intention which cannot be realized. Without reciprocity no common life can be established between us. Further, the intention to be friends, even if it is mutual, does not itself constitute fellowship; it constitutes merely the condition of its possibility. Fellowship has to be realized in the activities of a common life, under material as well as psychological conditions which vary continually. It has to be lived through difficulties, and the difficulties have to be overcome. But provided the intention is maintained on both sides, some realization of fellowship and of freedom is certain, and some common life is necessarily established. But its quality depends upon the extent to which the fear of the other —which is the fear for the self—is overcome in practice and not merely in intention. Fellowship has to be lived: it cannot be established once for all. For though the activities of a common life may persist through habit after the intention of a fellowship has ceased, the unity which remains is no longer a fellowship but only a co-operation for common purposes.

We had to concentrate our attention upon friendship, as the simplest and most fully realized example of human fellowship, in order to grasp the structural principles of the second type of unity which binds human beings together. We may now return to the more general aspects of human community, which are our immediate concern. It might be thought that a friendship between two people is such a unique and exclusive relation that it has little in common with those larger groups which we call communities. Friendship is a very personal and intimate thing, and no man can have more than a few real and lasting friends. This is, of course, true in fact, but the conclusion does not follow. Friendship, in this sense, is only the full realization, the ripe fruit of human fellowship, and it is, perhaps, even rarer than we are apt to think. But the root from which it springs, and the soil in which it grows, are universal. In particular, the intention which it fulfils is the same in all forms of fellowship, and it is this, as we have seen, that is decisive.

Since we can only be ourselves in fellowship, in a mutual caring for one another, it follows that the intention to enter into fellowship is implicit in every human being and in every human activity. This indeed is what makes us human. It is the positive ground-motive of all personal life, and so both absolutely basic and absolutely universal. *The ground of fellowship is common humanity*. It is not one intention among others, but the integrating intention which gives meaning to all the others, and to which they are relative. This means, in the concrete, that the natural tendency of any two human beings who meet one another is to enter into fellowship, irrespective of all differences, whether of age, sex, race, nationality, social condition, natural ability or any other, simply as human beings. If, in fact, they do not, it must be because the natural tendency is inhibited by fear. Any meeting of persons holds the potentiality of self-realization for all of them. Since this rests upon the basic structure of human personality, its objective correlate is a universal fellowship of persons, a single human community. This shows us the proper meaning of what is called 'love of humanity'. It is misunderstood if it is

construed as a thin, diffuse and rather sentimental attitude of general benevolence. Like all attitudes, it can be
sentimentalized, and then it is unreal. But in its proper
meaning the 'love of humanity' is simply the recognition
and explicit affirmation of the implicit intention which
constitutes our own personal nature. To love humanity
is not to feel a vague affection for some imaginary human totality. It is to maintain the disposition and the
purpose to care for *any* human being with whom we are
brought into relation, in whatever fashion circumstances
make possible, and simply on the ground of our common
humanity.

The primitive human community is the family—the
kinship group. It is also the original unit of co-operation.
The common life of co-operative activity is grounded in
fellowship, and stands in no need of organization so long
as the fellowship is unbroken. Now since human nature
is intentional, and not mere matter of fact, and since the
primary need is to maintain and perpetuate the fellowship, there must be a set of group activities designed to
express the consciousness and maintain the intention of
fellowship in a common life. These activities constitute
the religion of the group. Religion is thus the original
expression of the specifically human element in group
life, of the capacity for reflection, of that Reason which
distinguishes man from the brutes. The unity of a human
group, however primitive, is not mere fact. It is not
maintained by 'instinct' or mere natural impulse, but
by those informed and transformed by the consciousness
of them; by reflection; by knowledge; by intentionality.
The core of religion, from its very origin, is the 'celebra-

tion of communion'—the expression and glorification of the consciousness of fellowship. Since all the aspects and all the activities of the common life meet in this consciousness of fellowship—for they are its content—religion is all-inclusive. Its objective correlative is the whole content of human experience and human activity. In its central function, it brings to consciousness the implicit human intention of unity in fellowship—with its principles of equality and freedom. It maintains the intention in consciousness, deepens and strengthens it, and directs it towards its day to day realization in the co-operative activities of the group. As an expression of conscious reflection, it enlarges the field of fellowship in time; linking the living with their dead and with the generations unborn. In this way it creates the sense of the group as continuing through time, overcoming death and the fear of death, and laying the foundations of history. . . . This is the significance of ancestor-worship as a form of primitive religion. . . . It guides the intention of fellowship to its realization in co-operative activity, so giving rise to conscious techniques, to fertility rites and all forms of magic. In this field also it exhibits the extending and generalizing activities of reflection. It provides and enforces general techniques of relationship in the practical life which are valid for all its members, so laying the foundations of morality and law. Since the fellowship has to be realized under the conditions imposed by Nature, it provides a consciousness of Nature and the powers of Nature as objective conditions of practical fellowship, and directs the intentionality of the group towards them. . . . This is the significance of primi-

86

tive Nature worship.... Since it is concerned with intentionality, it has to *symbolize* its objectives; consequently its primary expressions are ritual activities in which all members of the community share. These religious rituals are parts of the common life; but they have a special characteristic which separates them from the other, ordinary parts, and which gives them an extraordinary character. They have a *meaning*: they refer beyond themselves, beyond the present immediacy of common experience, to what is not present. They *represent* what is hoped for, what is feared, what is purposed in common. So, on the subjective side, primitive religion is an awareness and enjoyment of fellowship, as well as an affirmation of it; while on its objective side it is a technique for the achievement of common intentions *through representation*. Religion is thus the matrix of all the representative activities of human consciousness, and of their rationality: of their rationality, because representation, as an activity of the imagination, is necessarily private and individual, and religion is concerned with community. So it involves the demand that the private activities of the imagination should conform to the conditions of community and be valid for all. Religion, then, is the original creator of *tradition*, which is the total common awareness of the group, as a persisting community. Tradition includes, on its practical side, awareness of the rules and techniques which are valid for maintaining the common life both as co-operation and as fellowship; and on its reflective side, a mythology which is valid for all its members, an orthodoxy of common belief. In this mythology two elements are fused which are the roots

87

of knowledge and art respectively. The first is a community of belief about the natural world, that is to say, about the persistent conditions under which the common life is carried on. The other is a set of common beliefs about what is to be hoped, feared, desired and intended, a set of symbolic expressions of the common emotions of the group. In this way common values are determined which regulate the intentional activities of the community, providing common grounds of priority in its choices.

There is no need to go further into the philosophy of religion. The point that concerns us is already sufficiently clear. Because of its central function of expressing the conscious and intentional unity of a human group, religion is necessarily the matrix and the generating source of all culture; that is to say, of all rational awareness, whether in its practical or its reflective aspects. In primitive religion all the aspects are held in solution, as it were, and fused together. When, in the development of religion, they are separated out, distinguished and contrasted with one another, they gain a relative autonomy, and form the basis of a division of labour in the community which is not merely economic. But they are still elements in the activity of a unified fellowship, and the consciousness of the fellowship, which religion primarily expresses, permeating the individual members of the community irrespective of their special functions, maintains a unity of spirit in all the aspects of their activity, and so a unity of culture; a tradition of common life. But in this case the unity of the group as a fellowship depends wholly upon the adequate fulfilment of the religious function; upon the maintenance and reinforcement of the consciousness of fellowship. In proportion as this fails, the unity of the group sinks to a mere habit of co-operation, which, though it may persist for a time by its own inertia, is bound to break up. For the autonomy of the elements of the common life becomes absolute, and the development of each is unrelated to that of the others. In their unqualified autonomy, they come into conflict and antagonism, as special interests, and divide society into competing and conflicting groups. The society itself would go into dissolution very quickly, were it not maintained by fear. The political function becomes paramount, and maintains co-operation by law and the threat of penalties. The more the habit of co-operation, the practical element in tradition, breaks down, the more unity of co-operation must be imposed and the more dictatorial government must become. Political leadership may, and almost certainly will, try to perform the religious function as well as its own, but the effect can only be spurious. For the political intention is co-operation, and it seeks to create fellowship for the sake of co-operation. This, as we have seen, is in the nature of things impossible, and the attempt is irrational. Friendship cannot be organized. Whatever the eventual outcome, freedom is lost; not merely freedom in fellowship but also, and as a gradual consequence, political freedom also.

Certain aspects of the development of religion demand our attention, however, because of their pertinence to our main theme. The first is the discovery of the inherent universality of religion, and the rise of 'universal' religions. Primitive religion is exclusive. It is the religion of a 'kinship group', and is limited to the 'kin'. We have already noticed the confusion of the organic relation of kinship with the personal unity of fellowship. This is natural in primitive society, for two reasons: firstly, because primitive society is as nearly organic as any human group can be, and secondly, because the natural family provides the environment within which personal relationships can most easily be established and maintained. But in the development of society the inclusion in the group of members who are not related by blood, through fusion, through inter-marriage or in any other fashion, has the effect of distinguishing between the organic and the personal unities. Men who are not related by blood behave 'like brothers'. So 'brotherhood' acquires a metaphorical meaning, by no means either sentimental or mystical, and comes to denote the state of being in fellowship, and religion becomes the expression of a consciousness of community irrespective of kinship, and borrows the terminology of kinship for a new and personal use.

When this distinction has been made, religion becomes potentially universal. When its implications are realized in reflection, the idea of a universal religion emerges. In the fullness of time, when the social pressures demand it, universal religions are founded. They are founded by individual persons, of high religious insight, who seek a personal community denied or frustrated by the character of the societies of which they are members, and who seek to realize the potential universality of personal fellowship. Only three of these religions have been permanently effective—Buddhism, Christianity and Islam—and remain to-day competitors for the universal allegiance of mankind. They are differentiated by the types of motivation which underlie them, and which provide the motive force of their expansion. In both Buddhism and Islam the negative motive is dominant. We noticed earlier that the dominance of fear has two expressions: one a withdrawal into the self from the other; the second an aggressiveness directed against the other. Buddhism seeks a universal fellowship through withdrawal from the enmities and dissensions which frustrate personal fellowship in the actual world. Islam seeks it through aggression and compulsion. Christianity, on the other hand, is positively motived. It seeks a universal fellowship realized in the actual conditions of human life, a brotherhood of mankind, a kingdom of heaven *on earth*.

It is, of course, obvious enough that in its long history Christianity has failed to maintain the characteristic intention of its foundation. Fear gets the upper hand and it falls into negation. But what is characteristic is that whether the failure tends, Buddhist fashion, to the escapism of a withdrawal from the world into a 'pure spirituality' or contrariwise, into the aggressive self-defence which, as in Islam, would use power to conquer the world, either of these aberrations is recognized, within the Christian fellowship itself, as a denial of its true nature, and produces a protest and a compensation. In the same way its tendency to become, in one or other of its branches, the religion of a limited group—a national religion, for example—is compensated for by a missionary movement which protests against exclusiveness. Its fundamental positiveness gives it a power of self-renewal which recalls it, after every aberration, to its original intention.

This original intention can, of course, be most easily discovered in the teaching of Jesus. Unfortunately, this teaching is usually misconstrued because it is interpreted in terms of a Graeco-Roman tradition which is alien to its own Hebrew background. Jesus presupposes the validity of the Hebrew conception of community in principle, as against the Roman type of society based upon law and administration backed by force. He stands with the tradition of his own people, for a human fellowship issuing in and conditioning social co-operation in every field. His own contribution to the development of Hebrew experience is rooted in a very clear consciousness of the personal character of any human fellowship, and the recognition that it has no essential relation to natural kinship. The parable of the Good Samaritan is a definite assertion that the basis of human relationship is common humanity. It follows that human fellowship is potentially universal, overriding all natural differences and all artificial grounds of exclusiveness: and that the implicit goal of human intentionality is the realization, in concrete experience, of an inclusive and total human fellowship, a brotherhood of mankind. But this is merely the starting point. The problem it sets is a realistic and practical one. How is the universal fellowship to be created?

The question, I repeat, is realistic and practical. There is a tendency in many quarters to think that it is idealistic and impractical, because it would involve a universal perfection of character which is far beyond the reach of the mass of human beings. Such a view rests upon an elementary misunderstanding of the relation between theory and practice. Any theory is ideal, and provides a standard which can never be fully realized in its application. One does not say that because ideal justice cannot be realized on earth, we should not aim at justice in the political field. We do not scorn the theory of the steam-engine because a perfect steam-engine cannot be built. Nor do we imagine that because an ideal friendship is beyond our capacity, it is stupid to make friends. The question of a universal community is of the same sort. If we understand the general principles which govern any human fellowship, we can ask the practical question, 'What conditions must be fulfilled by any actual community if it is to extend without limits and so become an inclusive fellowship?'

What is often referred to as the 'ethical teaching of Jesus' is a realistic attempt to answer this question. The background is the Roman Empire and its drive towards a universal and inclusive State, based upon legal justice and efficient administration, and achieved by aggression. The Hebrew community, to which Jesus belongs, rests upon an antithetical principle of unity, and must reject the Roman Empire in principle. The Roman State has no inner unity. It is not a fellowship. If, as a Jew, Jesus must reject the Roman Empire, he must also accept the principle of universality—of a kingdom of heaven on earth—which is implicit in the Hebrew tradition. What, then, is the alternative? The Roman city-state has expanded into a universal State in its fashion, according to its own principles. How can the limited Hebrew community expand to a universal community in accordance with *its* own principles? In particular, what conditions must it fulfil in order that this may be possible?

The general conditions to be fulfilled are those which constitute a unity of fellowship in contrast to a mere unity of co-operation. These we have already considered. But we must add a new condition, the intention of universality. The expansion of the Roman State to universality sets the problem of the expansion of a limited community to universality. Clearly such an expansion cannot be based upon aggression, and cannot appeal to fear. The very nature of fellowship renders such methods self-stultifying. The alternative rests upon the principle that fellowship between persons is natural, and will be realized wherever fear is overcome. Consequently, the technique for the expansion of a fellowship—if one may use such a phrase—must be a technique for eliminating fear. This enables us to understand the principle of 'forgiveness' which Jesus substitutes for 'punishment' in dealing with injury, or the injunction to 'love one's enemies'. These are, in fact, the conditions of reconciliation; and granted the intention of universal fellowship, they follow of necessity as practical rules for its achievement.

The exclusion of fear, as the principle of a fellowship which intends universality, has both an internal and an external reference. Internally, the fellowship must be constituted in such a fashion that it is *potentially* universal. It must, in principle, be open to everyone, and therefore no principle which differentiates between people, such as race, sex, nationality or creed, must enter into its constitution. Since its constitution is psychological, is the structure of its common mind, this means that it is not on the defensive. It does not seek to defend its exclusive individuality against other groups or individuals. It must be prepared to lose its life as this particular community in order to find it again in a more inclusive community.

Externally, it is not afraid of those who are outside its membership, whether they are individuals or groups. Since it intends universality, all men are potentially members of it. They are outside only because they exclude themselves; and they exclude themselves because they are afraid. The problem of achieving their inclusion is the problem of overcoming the fear which excludes them. How is this to be done? Evidently it can only be achieved if the community which seeks to include them in its fellowship is one of which no one can rightly be afraid. It must neither withdraw into itself nor become aggressive against others: and it must maintain this attitude, under all circumstances, in its relations with outsiders. The critical issue arises over its attitude to aggression against itself. For its refusal to defend itself invites aggression, and provides the conditions for successful aggression. The group which intends universality is committed to pacifism. The reason for this should be carefully noticed. It is the only means to achieve its end; for if it resists it abandons its purpose. Moreover, there is no guarantee that its pacifism will be successful in any particular instance. The justification of its refusal to resist evil lies in the belief that the fear which motivates aggression is illusory and self-stultifying; and this is so only because its own refusal to resist is not a means of self-defence, not a withdrawal from co-operation, not a mere submissiveness grounded on fear. It is only the negative aspect of its offer of friendship and co-operation, of its care for the other party and for the interests of the other party. The pacifism which is a weapon of self-defence, since it rests on fear, justifies the fear which lies behind aggression, and cannot hope to eliminate it.

Such are the principles which dictate the behaviour of any limited fellowship which intends a universal fellowship. We must not forget, however, that as statements of principle they are necessarily ideal. They are the norms for conduct which aims at a community which shall be all-inclusive. When we apply them to the actual conditions of human life, we shall expect them to involve a simplification of the actual issues. In the light of this we may restate the conclusion as follows. Firstly, any fellowship which intends the creation of a universal human community will tend to be successful in so far as it behaves in accordance with these principles, and will tend to fail in so far as it abandons them. Secondly, in so far as any community actually behaves in accordance with these principles it will tend to create a universal community. We have to combine these two assertions for the reason that a group may intend universality and yet fail to achieve it by using means that are incompatible with its intention; and also it may tend to produce universality by behaving in a way that has this effect, without consciously intending a universal fellowship.

It has been necessary to discuss the teaching of Jesus in this way, and to this extent, because it has a direct bearing upon the problem of human freedom as it faces us to-day. The Christian churches are the outcome of the life and teaching of Jesus. The Hebrew community to whom Jesus appealed to undertake the task was not prepared to sink its individual identity in a universal fellowship. It was left to the small group of his followers to become the nucleus of the self-expanding fellowship which he envisaged; and this original group, in its international expansion, became the Christian Church, and the historic instrument for the creation of a community expanding towards the community of mankind.

No one who is seriously concerned about the future of freedom can afford to overlook or to under-estimate Christianity. To maintain and increase human fellowship is the function of religion; and the achievement of an inclusive human fellowship is a religious task. To this task the Christian fellowship is committed by its origin and its history. However much it may forget or falsify the intention of its foundation, or fail to realize the conditions of its achievement, it is tied both to the teaching of its founder and to the hope and purpose of a fellowship of common humanity. As a result it is subject always to criticism, both from within and from without, which reminds it of its principles and recalls it to its function. It is this criticism, no doubt, which explains its extraordinary capacity for renewal and reform. It created the inner unity both of western and of eastern

Europe, and as a result it underlies the two traditions which to-day tend to divide the world between them in a struggle for political dominion. In the recent past, through its missionary enterprises, it has established itself in all the great centres of the world's population, and everywhere exerts an influence far in excess of its numerical strength. When we add to this the indirect effects of its civilizing influence through the centuries, we are bound to conclude not merely that it is a significant factor in the problem that faces civilization, but that there is no other factor which can rival it in importance. In a very real and practical sense it is the only instrument for the achievement of a community of the world which we possess. If this is not obvious to us, it is because we think so completely in terms of organization and engineering; in terms appropriate only to the political task of enlarging and consolidating the unity of co-operation by means of law, backed always, as it must be if it is to be effective, by force. For this task religion has no aptitude. Its function is a different one, and its end dictates quite different methods.

We can sum up the general argument, however, without special reference to Christianity, in this way. A universal community would be one in which, in fact, all men are potentially friends. By this is meant that they do in fact care for one another in their actual relations, whatever these may be; that when brought into direct relations they act as friends and enter into fellowship. For this to be possible two conditions are necessary—an intention in them all to behave in this fashion, and a common way of life that is shared by all. All intention depends for its realization upon habit; and what we call a 'way of life' is simply a system of social habit. The achievement of a fellowship of mankind waits upon the creation of a way of life that is common to all men everywhere, and which would replace the various divergent ways of life which differentiate the humanity of to-day, and prevent mutual understanding. The old traditions everywhere are breaking down. The task before us is to lay the foundations of a single tradition for the world as a whole. Now a tradition is the embodiment, in the habits of common life, of a system of values. The incompatibility of different traditions is brought about by the inclusion of values which discriminate between people in terms of natural or artificial differences, between white and black, for instance, or between rich and poor, or between educated and uneducated. A universal tradition could only be grounded in the habit of treating all men as persons. Common humanity would be its basis of judgment, respect for personality its first law, and friendship, which is the fullest realization of the personal life, its supreme good, to which all other goods are subordinate.

It remains only to point the moral of a long discussion by returning to its central theme—the conditions of freedom of our own day. The necessity of our time is the achievement of an effective world-order. This is not simply a desirable step forward in human progress. It is a necessity from which we cannot escape and in face of which we have no choice. We shall move from war to war, from catastrophe to catastrophe until somehow it is achieved. There is no effective alternative. The condition of freedom from now onwards is bound up with this. The effort to maintain the limited freedoms of our traditional, isolated communities, if we do no more than this, is futile. They will continue to dwindle away, or to be violently suppressed, as they are doing, unless we can universalize them. We have to establish freedom for all men in a single world order, or lose our own.

Most of those who realize this—and they are many—tend to envisage the problem as a political one, to be solved through economic and legal organization on a global scale. They look for some kind of world state to emerge from the international conferences of exalted statesmen or through the development of the United Nations Organization and its associated agencies, or through the triumph of communism, or in some other fashion, according to the political ideal which they favour. But these competing ideals are incompatible. Consequently the efforts to realize them are thwarted, and become efforts to prevent the other party from realizing theirs. The effort to realize a communist world order is transposed into an effort to prevent, by all means, the achievement of a democratic world order, and vice versa. Political action everywhere is driven into negation and stultified.

It has been one of the main purposes of this book to reveal the reason for this tragic stultification of international politics in our time. The efforts which have been made to achieve international agreement since the end of the first world war have been without parallel in history. They have not merely failed of their object; they have made the situation progressively worse. Why do our efforts to organize world peace carry us from one world war to another? Why do our attempts to reach international agreement sharpen disagreement into hatred, and become milestones on the road to catastrophe?

The answer we have found is that we are asking of the politician what politics by its nature can never achieve. The State is concerned, in its positive functions, with the unity of co-operation. It organizes, with law as its instrument, the co-operative activities of men for the achievement of common purposes. It requires and enforces conformity to law. But the unity of fellowship, because it is unorganizable, because it is necessarily spontaneous and spiritual, lies outside its scope. We have seen that a unity of co-operation may be the expression of a unity of fellowship; but it need not be. So the State may be the instrument of fellowship; the means to the expression, in common activities, of a true community. Where this is so the organizing task of government is easy: but in proportion to the absence of fellowship it becomes more difficult and more oppressive. In particular, it is only so far as the State is an expression of fellowship that it can be an instrument of justice, and of freedom through justice. We had forgotten that law is not necessarily justice. In the hands of a Hitler it can be an instrument of injustice and despotism. If those who are governed are not in fellowship, if they do not care for one another, but only for themselves, then a bare unity of co-operation is all that can be achieved. The State becomes absolute, and its aim, unqualified by the control of fellowship, reveals itself as a rational efficiency. Neither justice nor freedom belongs to the essence of politics. They derive from the personal fellowship of the common life, and are added to the political life. Where there is no fellowship, there can be neither freedom nor justice, or only such justice as is expedient. It is precisely because the proper and natural purpose of politics is the efficient organization of co-operation that the price of freedom is eternal vigilance. The temptation to gain efficiency at the expense of freedom is always present.

The achievement of an efficient unity of world co-operation is indeed a political task. It is *the* political task of the present day. But if we commit it wholly to the politicians, if we forget the task of extending fellowship as co-operation extends; if we neglect the agencies whose function it is to enlarge the boundaries of fellowship—religion above all—and the partial agencies which derive from it and share its aim and spirit, then we ought not to be surprised if the achievement of a world polity is accompanied by the loss of freedom everywhere. We ought not to be amazed if it should come as the result of another and more terrible world war. A military dictatorship of the world, with scientific instruments of terrorization sufficient to make resistance futile, would be a solution of the political task, if that is all that we demand: and it is not difficult to imagine conditions arising, in the near future, which would make it preferable, for the mass of mankind, to an international anarchy which produced famine. Under Augustus, the Roman Empire did just this for the civilization of its time, and the peace it imposed, and the international co-operation it achieved, were hailed as a boon in its own day and are still held up for admiration in ours.

This may well be the solution of the impasse we have reached which history has in store for us. But to any individual or nation for whom freedom is the pearl of great price, it is a bitter prospect. It would mean that the struggle for freedom would have to start again from the beginning. Within the world-empire, we should find ourselves in the same position as the Jews within the Roman Empire in the time of Christ; facing the same problem of transforming a world co-operation into a world fellowship. The conditions under which this could be accomplished would still be those which he discovered, expressed, and exemplified in his life and death. The Christian Church would still be the only existing institution capable of undertaking the task, which is, indeed, its historic mission and the justification of its existence.

But however probable such a solution may seem, it is not inevitable. The balance of motives in human society is incalculable, and its transformations are apt to be sudden and unexpected. The manifestations of fear are more spectacular than those of love and trust, so that we tend to over-estimate their relative power. Evil is parasitic upon good; the negative forces in personal life ultimately draw their strength from the positive forces, so that there are natural limits which they cannot pass. It may be that there is already in the world a sufficient basis of fellowship to produce and sustain an agreed solution, even if, at first, it is a precarious agreement, constantly threatened, and upheld through crisis after crisis only with difficulty. We do not and we cannot know. We can discover only in the attempt. Since this is so there is only one proper course for all, whether individuals or nations, who love freedom. It is to strive in every field and at every opportunity for world unity by agreement; and against the temptation, however strong, to appeal to force or the threat of force. But we should not deceive ourselves. We must be realists. Success cannot be guaranteed, and the signs are against it. The appeal to force does offer a solution; but only at the expense of freedom.

Prophecy, however, even if it were possible, is undesirable. What is important is to understand, and then to fulfil, the conditions of human freedom in our time: and since our necessity is world unity, these conditions are, at last, even as a matter of practical politics, the conditions of freedom for all men. The critical point of our discussion is the conclusion that the basic conditions of freedom lie outside the political field, and cannot be produced or maintained by any ingenuity of statecraft; though a perverted politics may disregard them even when they are present, and can do much to destroy them. Freedom is the product of human fellowship, and the laws of friendship are its conditions. These conditions are spiritual, moral, religious: that is to say, they depend upon the motives that animate men in their personal relations with one another. The struggle for freedom is the struggle for the transformation of human motives, for the triumph of friendship over mistrust, of love over fear. Politics is necessary to freedom; the more necessary the larger is the society which it embraces.

FREEDOM IN FELLOWSHIP

But a democratic polity is possible only for a human community which has established a common way of life upon a basis of mutual trust; and the extent and quality of the freedom it provides depends upon the extent to which those it governs and organizes are in communion with one another.

If we realize that there is not one form of human unity but two; that law enforced by a state is not the only unifying principle in human relationship, then we see that the possibilities of a world unity are not limited to the construction of a world state on the model of the nation states of to-day. I confess that I find the dream of a super-state governing the whole world something of a nightmare, even when it presents itself in the garments of federalism. The States we know are as they are largely because they are exclusive and have to face outwards, armed to the teeth, to defend their exclusiveness and sovereign independence. In a world fellowship the barriers of nationalism could be down, and their political implications would vanish with them. We should be free to draw such boundaries on the map as were most convenient for the purposes of co-operative activity; and the co-ordination of these units of political organization, in so far as that was necessary, and for this special purpose or that, could be arranged without difficulty, without the need for a single sovereign centre of power which should be omnicompetent. If anyone thinks this the idle dream of visionaries, he should consider the extent to which it has actually been achieved, even under existing conditions, within the fellowship of the British Commonwealth.

FREEDOM IN FELLOWSHIP

So we return to our starting point. Freedom is our nature. But our nature lies always beyond us, and has to be intended and achieved. The obstacle lies in our fear, and the craving for security which expresses it. So at every crisis we are faced with a free choice between freedom and security. If we choose security, and make that our aim, we lose freedom, and find in the end that security eludes us. If we choose freedom, then we are debarred from aiming at security; for that would mean imposing our bondage upon others. If we choose freedom we may find the security we do not seek, though of this there can be no guarantee: yet it is the only path that offers promise of security. The generosity which offers friendship to others commits itself to their goodwill. They may respond in kind; perhaps we have grounds for believing that in the long run the response must come if we have the patience to wait and to persist. Of the immediate response we cannot be certain and the long run may be very long. Yet it is simple realism to recognize that there is no other way to freedom, if it is indeed freedom that we seek. Freedom is conditional, and these are its conditions. It is for those, whether individuals or peoples, who are ready to pay its price.